Flywheels
of Interdependence

By Fred Pierre

Copyright © 2024 Fred Pierre
All rights reserved.
ISBN: 979-8-9917755-0-2

DEDICATION

Friends by Fred Pierre / Chris Ballew collab

Thanks to the Last Exit Poets for encouraging me to write. Special thanks to Wick Poetry Center Director David Hassler for challenging me to read aloud in front of a group. Thanks to my family for supporting me in my writing efforts. Thanks to my friends who listened to my poems and encouraged me. This is a work of love, dedicated to everyone who loves. We can fix this broken world. Love is the glue.

Acknowledgements

Fred read **Everything** for Outdoor Voices in an Indoor World: Volume 6 on You Tube, April 30, 2021.

Toil Not and Neither Spin appeared in Tiny Seed Journal, May 10, 2021.

A prose version of **All Swim Free** was published in Tiny Seed Journal, January 31, 2022.

The Lighthouse of Maracaibo and **Beat Box** were published in The Elevation Review #7, National Poetry Month Issue, April 2022.

Pandora's Book appeared in Tiny Seed Journal, November 22, 2022.

Paella appeared in Culinary Origami, Edition 1 - Winter Issue, March 2023.

The Illusion of Permanence appeared in Overtly Lit, Issue 3, June 2023.

Phantasm and **Numerology** appeared in The Locust Review, Issue 10, October 5, 2023, print and online.

bark! was published in the Dear Maj chapbook, April 8, 2024, Last Exit Press.

CONTENTS

Preface 7
Love Woven Into the Fabric 11
The River 25
Heart Home 29
Numerology 51
The Epic of Scághaich 63
Green Mother 79
Everything 99
Your Dark Branches 105
Beat Box 115
Why Can't We See Our Oppressor? 139
Horizons 149
Poem for Akarya Charaka 169
Liquidity 179
Love Born at the Co-op 187
Poems for Parvati 193
Running Wild 209
Gospel of the Flowers 217

Cover art and illustrations by Fred Pierre.

Preface

This poetry collection grew out of a project called Gospel of the Flowers, a series of poems based on the wheel of the year, with poetry spanning Summer, Autumn, Winter and Spring. I imagined that flowers might have their own bible and these poems would be the verses. G.O.T.F. poems channel creation myths to investigate floral mysteries.

Beat Box is an attempt to evade logical structure and to focus on the rhythm and melody of poetry. Beat Box is set in the North Beach, west of San Francisco, where Diane di Prima has just finished reading Revolutionary Letter #9.

My Scághaich and Akarya project encompassed four long poems: The Epic of Scághaich, The River, Everything, and Poem for Akarya Charaka. I have repurposed these long poems as interludes between groups of shorter poems.

Why Can't We See Our Oppressor is a tribute to Shoshanna Zuboff and an elaboration on the concepts explored in her groundbreaking book, The Age of Surveillance Capitalism.

FLYWHEELS

Love Born at the Co-op is about meeting my wife, Amie, while volunteering at my local, food co-op, where I studied herb lore and found food freedom.

The Last Exit Poets host a monthly reading at the bookstore in Kent. I enjoy performing spoken word, so I'm motivated to write poems each month for the reading. I jot down ideas on napkins, talk into my phone and assemble favorite lines from my journal.

Rhythm is important to me, but I don't count syllables. I sound the phrases out in my head and adjust the wording for cadence.

I begin this collection with Friend, because it's one of my favorite poems to perform. Can we learn peace from a pair of hawks and can a friendship be sustained across disputed borders? Quiet images of nature contrast with the thoughtlessness of war.

Have you ever wondered where lightning strikes the most? While I performed The Lighthouse of Maracaibo for open mic hip-hop night at the Standing Rock Cultural Arts Gallery, Kent State's homecoming fireworks boomed like a million thunderclouds, punctuating my verses like lightning strikes as we dashed out to watch the sky light up.

Sick with Covid in 2020, I searched the internet for advice from Ayurvedic practitioners. A common recommendation was to drink Tulsi Tea (also known as Holy Basil). It warms your core and stimulates inner fire, called agni. In the process, I learned about the wandering scholar, known as Akarya Charaka, who wrote the first treatise on Ayur-Ved. The Poem for Akarya Charaka is long, but so is the Ayur-Ved. I love it's ideas and language.

Scághaich has been called Ireland's greatest woman warrior. With her diabolical spear, the Gáe Bulg, she and her troops laid waste to armies. When Scághaich was asked to serve justice on Queen Maeve for stealing a sacred cow, it began an epic struggle between light and darkness, like an Irish Tao-te-ching, resulting in a unique creation story.

Emergent Being and the Birth of Love mine Greek, Norse and Maori myths to speculate about creating something from nothing, when Earth emerged from the void, aka the Mystery, known as Ginnungap in Norway and Te Kore in Maori tradition.

I wrote bark! about my dog who passed, but it was much-loved Kent poet, Maj Ragain who coined the phrase, "Be a Love Dog."

FLYWHEELS

This poetry project started when I asked successful poetry instigator and Kent State Wick Poetry Center director, David Hassler, why people read poetry out loud. He said simply, "Try it." That was 2019.

With shaking hands and a quavering voice that became stronger as I read, I presented my first poem at the Last Exit bookstore in Kent. Adrenaline coursed through my body and I felt elated. It was thrilling. Now I perform poetry every chance I get – at art openings, hip-hop jams, even the downtown Gazebo on a Saturday night. I still get a thrill every time, but my hands don't shake as much and I've learned to engage with my audience.

My influences for Flywheels include Mary Oliver, John Muir, Diane di Prima, Adrienne Marie Brown, Joy Harjo, Thich Nhat Than, Tibetan / Bon legends, Buddhist sutras and ancient Greek myths.

Why are there so many love poems woven into this collection? Because love is important in a world gone slightly mad. Love has intrinsic value in a world where dreams and desires are monetized. In the holistic energy body, love is what heals us all. I call upon the gods and goddesses of love to weave us all into a colorful, social fabric.

FLYWHEELS

Love Woven Into The Fabric

FLYWHEELS

Friend

my friend
your country and my country
are divided by war
while we play together
while we love each other

the wind blows in change
we transition to wind
the Indra-net's sustainable
cultural values

I lay on my back
and look up at the sky
there's a river of birds flying over
they follow the water in vast murmuration
below me the river flows on

two vultures in love
they always fight fair
two hawks care for each other
together they
polish the moon

FLYWHEELS

I dream twin doppelgangers,
One says "I'm the imposter"
The reply is
"No I'm the imposter"

it's hard to find people without any flaws
so meet folks wherever they are
call out bad behavior
condemn the race to oblivion
and sow peace in restorative justice

your country and my country
forever scarred by this war
while we play together
while we care for each other
my friend

FLYWHEELS

Love is My Religion

Love is my religion.
May it also be yours.

Sometimes it's tough love,
And sometimes it's disaster,
But mostly it's valuing others,
By forgetting myself for a moment.

With love as a broom,
I can clean up the world.
Real love speaks the truth,
Joy, ecstatic, transforms.

Are we riders of love,
Or are we the ridden?
Bodies merge as we ride
On the trail south of Spirit.

There's no doubt love enchants,
So become it's enchantress
Your touch transforms the world.
So much better because you are in it.

FLYWHEELS

Enlightenment

when you learn
the system's set up to consume you,
you bite the hand
that's been feeding you.
you find a new way,
and you put it to practice.
Freedom's the only way forward.

In rebellion
Every time you volunteer
Your intention starts something.
You make change
When you act with compassion.

How much of yourself
Can you give?
Go all in.
Love and Life
Want to give it all back!

FLYWHEELS

String Theory

Imagine an orchestra played by the stars.
Where time is a string set aquiver.
Cosmic choirs let fly with canticular arrows.
Vocal valor achieves the heart's bullseye.

The vacuum catastrophe's not unexpected,
Zero-point on the last train to Hooverville.
Plumb the emptiness, sip on unlimited bandwidth,
We'll renew and revive our connection.

Love unfurls its wings as it's called into being,
Dormant long in the fabric of time.
Now I've fallen prey to love's patient mechanics.
Quantum entanglement never lets go.

The Birth of Love

The goddess of love, Aphrodite,
Was born from the sea foam of heaven.

Darkest night birthed golden-winged Eros,
Who preached gospels of passion and desire.
From Aphrodite and Eros emerged golden Agape:
Unconditional, transcendent love.

Aristophanes says Eros impregnated Chaos to create
A winged template for the birth of all birds.

We all birth amour and amitié,
Love conditionally and unconditionally,
Romantically and affectionately, and
Seek refuge in the jewel that,
"No matter whom you love we welcome you."

FLYWHEELS

My Triumphant Return from the Virtual

We'll explore life within us,
Where there are no limits.
Time holds space for you here,
By Earth's love you are blessed.

Today we will feast,
Mother Earth will provide,
Spring greens and ramps,
Spinach, peas and arugula.

Goldfinch chats, egrets crossing the towpath,
They are gathering sticks for an eyrie.
Muskrat whiskers crease the canal.
Red-winged blackbirds exclaim the ecliptic.

Mankind's pride knows no limits,
There are things to be proud of,
But today our assumptions are challenged.
We depend on the real, but inhabit the virtual.

You can unplug the internet,
But Nature's batteries last,
They are charged with unstoppable sunshine.

FLYWHEELS

Love's display is a spectrum.
Be the rainbow! You are all of the colors.
Be magnanimous sharing your wavelengths.
Wisdom's strength is in patience.
The rebirth of the Earth we await.

Earth is not an experiment.
This Spring fall in love,
With Nature and her recurrent cycle.
Our star's brilliant sunlight and benign gravity,
Host an infinite well of potential.

Love Battery

Our love is a battery that powers the stars.
I believe in my heart that across millions of
   light years,
Creatures of mystery and brilliance care for
   each other.
Equanimity and compassion enacted all
   of creation.
When Mystery gave birth to Love.

FLYWHEELS

Castaway

Your skin feels soft as it welcomes my touch.
My arm fits the length of your thigh and my hand
    hugs the curve of your hip.
Your lips brush my chest.
    Your tongue tickles my ear.
Your breath smells like islands,
    scent floral and sweet.
On your beach the waves crash
    and gulls call.
I sail where your skin maps my heart's buried treasure.
Loving you is my predestination.

Sailing the Ocean of Measureless Joy

The zephyr skips across the waves,
Scent of distant islands like
An aphrodisiac thunderbolt.

We'll study how Wind connects us over time,
Sound of wind as it blows through the leaves
 and the branches,
In the outbreath pause there is infinite potential.

Love uplifts us.
Love is like that.
It raises all boats.

FLYWHEELS

The Illusion of Permanence

You cannot tether the wind.
You can't hold on to lightning.
Crisis stimulates tragedy's pull.

Welcome to a world that's completely chaotic.
In these moments, god comes out to play.
They want you to believe that the world's lost it's magic,
But mundanity hosts profound miracles.

Love unfolds in the detail,
Supersedes superstructure.
All you need is love
sparked between moments.

Search too hard, you won't find it,
Can't find it? Then pledge
to Soul's eternal promise,
 "Love…Let it Be Here Now."

FLYWHEELS

The Flower Bed

We share a flower bed.
You bloom at night and
release your magnificent scent.
I'm falling into you and
I'm on gravity's side.

You fascinate me with your colors.
Fertilize me with your vision.
Gathered into your root embrace.
We interweave blossoms.

Let us cultivate growth,
As we harvest desire.
I'll mend my broken stems.
Your compassion's my soil.

Our love reflects cosmic connection,
Emergent in the fabric of time.
Threads of goddess are woven in everything,
Stitch inseparable causality.

FLYWHEELS

Ignite

We share a smile,
Fall in love with wild abandon.
New love sparkles and shines,
Won't see the scratches until we get closer.

Will our love become a list of grievances, or
Evolve into daily devotion,
A prayer and a delicate crafting.
Will our love transform us into a polished jewel,
That is at once both flawed and flawless?

Our love tends a fire whose coals never die,
Inner heat warms my core through cold winters.

Pandora's Book

I opened Pandora's seed library.
Let go of my fears about dirt.
I have no doubt hope and love will work magic,
Revealed in a tiny, green sprout.

FLYWHEELS

FLYWHEELS

The River

FLYWHEELS

The River
The river is potential,
Energy of uplift source.
Go with the flow they say, I do.
Yet to swim upstream, against the flow,
Is surely noble too.

A river's art is waterfalls.
Stones surrender to erosion.
In the river, one rock stands alone,
With petrified devotion.

Blue heron stalks quicksilver prey,
Under the cascade sheets,
Potent, timeless as a monolith,
Until her energy's unleashed.

Men rush in where herons halt.
Death stalks us from above.
Return upstream to placid pools,
Of indefatigable love.

FLYWHEELS

Endless waters, ever-changing,
Hidden swamps and swollen streams.
In oxbows quietly abandoned,
Float the relics of our dreams.

Surrender fear unto the river,
Never let it dam this flow.
From the hill down to the ocean,
See how quickly you can row.

To inundate this hydra,
Many heads combine each day,
I dive into the cleanest source,
Surface in toxic bay.

River bend suspends us softly,
In her cool, belov'd embrace.
They say the river splits our city,
But it binds us to this place.

Sunshine, water, bird and laughter,
Paint communities of sharing.
To inspire others to give back,
Build a bridge of active caring.

FLYWHEELS

To the river send your hopes,
Your art, your vision and your dreams,
Carried far beyond the ocean,
By this octopus of streams.

In our endless water cycle,
There will always be more rain.
We live in Erie's crescent.
Water is our middle name.

Circumfluent timeless flow,
Historic city, ancient trees.
Be a bird upon the water,
Or a creative honey bee.

FLYWHEELS

Heart Hearth
Earth **Home**

FLYWHEELS

Paella

Bring home a baguette,
To shop every day means its fresh.
I pass by the old men playing boules,
To frequent the boulanger.

My dad quit his job in insurance,
Apprenticed to a baker in Paris.
He learned to make Madeleine's,
The tiny cakes look like seashells.

Tomates Provençales,
How I hated tomatoes,
Stuffed with meat,
And with cheese and zucchini.

Grandpa Claude made his own wine,
And he pinched us too hard,
Fed the dog only table scraps,
But he let us swim in the cistern.

Suzette made paella with clams from the ocean,
In Provence guests do not go home hungry.
"Would you like more?" asked our host,
Though full, we will answer, "Merci."

FLYWHEELS

For me it was all about cocoa.
Toblerone, pain au chocolat.
The patisserie: Galettes and gateaus,
Eating sweets on the Champs-Elysees.

We climbed a stone stair in the
 crumbling monastery,
An abbey five hundred years old.
Afraid to be sucked into history's sand
Watched the ant lion seizing its prey.

As I stir a reduction of squash in my kitchen
I add cumin, lemon peel and paprika.
Will I pass cooking culture on down to my children?
Now the world is our recipe book.

FLYWHEELS

Del Mar

Listen to the wind
the traffic sounds like surf
I drift back in time
to my grandmother's porch
overlooking the ocean

I walked on the bluffs
down a path to the beach
seagulls circled and shrieked
the breeze fresh with the chorus
of a million wavelets

smell of salt
smell of kelp
even sand has a smell
the long waves repeating their call

dive in, dive in

this vast canvas of ocean
shimmers into the distance
like time
it feels like forever

FLYWHEELS

Grandma Louise slices fruit for breakfast
papaya and honeydew,
juice that she squeezed from an orange

every day I wake up to the waves and the gulls
nothing changes except the high tide line
tide is up
tide is down
but the ocean
still breaks on the rocks

all of the crabs understand this

FLYWHEELS

The Lighthouse of Maracaibo

Sailors of Venezuela
Set their course by the Beacon
That strobes above Lake Maracaibo.

The cascade Catatumbo pours into the lake,
That's surrounded on three sides by mountains.
Locals call it the River of Fire.
Every evening clouds roil,
And gather and thunder.
Lightning strikes like a viper,
On average, once every three seconds.

If you've ever gone down to the sea with me,
You know I navigate based on chaos.
The flickering gabble of unbroken storms,
Calls me home like an unholy choir.

Spray cross the bowsprit, I pull down the sail.
We are drifting in uncharted waters.
Fog blown by wind takes us in like soft fronds.
Pass in dream-light betwixt rocky islands,
Hungry monsters around us, abeyant.

FLYWHEELS

To know God's mind,
Please consider if you will for a moment,
The inevitable lightness of being.
Stars above, stars below,
Place your faith in the compass,
And over the waves you will go.

If you've ever gone down to the sea with me,
Then I wasn't alone or divisible.
I grant the crew leave to explore Baranquilla.
While I spiral into your zephyr,
Becalmed when,
I tell you my anchor is love.

Touch the Sky
I plumb deep blue sky for a message,
Leap laughing into awe and wonder.

Life's work plays out against a backdrop of purpose.
Wisdom flickers like a solitary lamp.
If you employ a concave mirror, it becomes
   a focused beacon.
To guide lost explorers home.

FLYWHEELS

The Bridge

Let a little light out
from your galaxies and stars
diamonds over and under
you came and comforted me.

Joy blew in, light refracted
in ice crystal droplets
rainbow blockworks
for all of life's stories.

A voluble heart supports
phenotic healing
To mend stems,
water generously.

Let's race sticks in the river,
so wide my mind follows
the current
on downstream, forever.

I run to the bridge.
You are already there.
We anticipate twigs,
as we watch the water pass under.

FLYWHEELS

All Swim Free

In that narrow strip between the road and the woods,
we search for the hidden entrance,
tucked in among the autumn olives and the poison ivy.

We dart in, ducking under vines,
Bullfrogs leap into the water as they sense
  our approach.
We're quieter, listening to the birds, frogs
  and katydids.
A cicada's buzz reaches a crescendo and fades
  into silence.

Among the reeds and bushes is a deep pool,
full of cool and clear water.
Back in the day, it was a fresh dig,
People fished from its shore.
Now nature is reclaiming the quarry.

Where the reeds end
is where the quarry drops off.
It's forty feet deep,
so it's best if you are a strong swimmer.

FLYWHEELS

I float on my back,
with my arms pointed over my head,
lungs full of air,
and I float without moving.
My feet rise when I fill my lungs,
and I'm like a raft on the ocean,
moved by the ripples and currents of the water.

There it is again,
the rumble of thunder,
this time more insistent.
There's a huge cloud approaching.
We dart and play in the water,
but our window to swim will close soon.

As we climb back up the steep side of the dig,
the wind shimmers in the cottonwood leaves.
It's a warm wind, but wild,
and the trees weave and twist.
The air is full of leaves,
spinning and whirling.
The cloud bursts.
Frogs crowd the path,
Because they love the rain.

FLYWHEELS

Then we're back through the bushes,
back on the road,
soaking wet as we run to the car,
Joyful for a glimpse of wild nature,
and thankful for a cooling swim.

FLYWHEELS

La Cigale Évitable

To value the future,
Set premonitions aside,
Surprise is our holy salvation.

Expect joy, expect pain?
I seek miracles daily,
Roadmaps only get you so far.

Our eyes express love.
One day I'll see your mouth.
Burst our bubbles by sharing a kiss.

Seventeen years your cicadas have slept
 in my garden.
Today's buzzsaw is my meditation.
I feel the sound waves within and around,

They vibrate right through me,
Circumventing all thought,
Their drone fills my entire perception.

Don't fuck with Science,
Because Science bites back.
Don't model actions you desire to prevent.

FLYWHEELS

Butterflies send a message with flowers,
Injustice anywhere impacts your life now,
Heaven's built upon faith in each other.

In a dynamic web strung from cause to effect.
Fear's answer is interdependence.
To survive here you'll have to trust others,

Listen warden,
I won't allow fear to enchain me.
Steadfast stand before oncoming storms.

To engage with my shadow is to leverage my truth,
What is courage besides being stubborn,
Not giving a fuck?
Only faith and commitment to principle.

Speak truth and become a role model.
Persistently shoulder life's burdens.
Remember the heart's a reliable touchstone.
The practice of kindness is love.

FLYWHEELS

One more Poem

Walk the path with heart my friend.
The God of Love is calling.
Life is communication.
Everything about you says freedom!

The fasces are sticks that gain strength when
  they're bundled.
Marks the judge with the power to kill.
Mussolini adopted fasces as his symbol,
Beat the people with sticks.
Rights suspended can only end badly.

Orion, tonight you're suspended in branches.
All night you will gift us with dreams.
To hunt with my dogs the elusive hart rampant.
Untethered in the forest of dreams.

In a live digiculture,
Where inclusion is priceless,
Van Neumann fear-machines
Iterate homegrown challenges,
Separation digs the roots of destruction.

FLYWHEELS

Why should I care how you dress,
Grow your hair, or what job you do,
Who do you love?
If we're sharing this moment of bliss?
Hot feet at the Scots' Tartan Dance-Off!

Love kills old selves,
When a new self is born.
From the helix that binds dust and shadow.

Proteins grown from dirt,
Weave our ravel complex,
To our horror, we unravel quickly.

Why worry about the werewolf?
The unaware wolf hunts daily,
Ignorance or irrational exuberance.

FLYWHEELS

connected

I wake up and connect
What's the news?
What is happening now?
Who said what?
Though my family's right here
We all have our screens
Net reliant
I retreat to the virtual

It feels like a
Drug or balm
For my brain
Overwhelming
Seductive
It beckons

I must face what is real alone
Alone, with no digital guidance
I feel vulnerable here
Until I connect
Then I'm powerful
My computational starship
Will sail the vast metaverse

FLYWHEELS

When Mystery Gave Birth to Love

Spirit of Mystery, we call on you.
God inhabits the Mystery.

Is love a warm energy fire,
That delicately opens all flowers?
A sun that enlightens our reason for being?

Or is love the cool force that binds galaxies?
An immense, gravitational power?
We've all fallen down it's well,
Laughing / Together.

It has been demonstrated that E equals MC squared.
Could love be the matter in the equation?
Is the fundamental layer of quantum mechanics,
a rubric to cultivate passion?

Am I your kryptonite? Or am I your fertilizer?
Love is patient. Love is kind. Love is nourishing.

You are a magical creature.
Sound and light bound together as beauty.
Where you love yourself is where I reside.
I stand I awe of your bravery,
Now is the time to claim your power!

Release the Empyrean

She's the coolest!
She's got style and confidence.
Her grin is infectious.

It's unselfconscious joy
and at the same time, pure mischief.
My own smile so wide
My brain's 'bout to topple.

> Your story grew into community.
> You help people define
> their relations to others.

> You're fair.
> You gave your opponent
> a chance to make peace.

> You don't fear to pass judgment,
> in life's biggest battles.
> You're courageous.
> You never back down.

> Cool works best for you,
> Being grounded, right here in the moment.
> Your chaos response is compassion.

FLYWHEELS

She's a buddhist of course.
Sees both sides of the issue.
Promotes kindness as the middle way.

Her motto's "Be here and enjoy it."
Superfluous thought isn't getting us anywhere.
She says be here now, let it be, and be grateful.

Her reaction time is the fastest on record.
Her body moves before her mind
　sends the command.
For a moment she's formless and then she resolves.

It makes her an intuitive dancer.
Acting goofy on the dance floor is one of her
　most adorable qualities.
She abandons all pretense, then she kicks out the jams.

> Joy itself is the intoxicant.
> Joy made of awe mixed with wonder
> Warming me as I stand by your fire.

Butterfly

Love inspires me
to seek you.
I catch sight of your face
of your body, your eyes and your form.
We will meet somewhere suddenly.
It happens quite often
When walking coincident paths
Serendipitous, yet unexplainable.
There you are.
You will smile.
You don't smile for everyone.
My heart will leap.
I'll run up and hold you
like I can hang on to you.
Obsession is oppression's cousin,
Once removed,
I remember my mission to free you.
I turn my palms to the sky,
Wings unfurl.
So beautiful when you take flight.

FLYWHEELS

Swimming Upstream by Fred Pierre

FLYWHEELS

FLYWHEELS

Numerology

FLYWHEELS

Time Crunch

Time runs from the hourglass.
Don't fall asleep on the job.
If the streets are too hot,
We'll go underground.
Way underground.

Who do you revere?
Are you faithful to influence?
A machine has been built to enslave you,
It steals our desires and sells them back
   as defective,
Fear's crescendo is its propaganda.

If something's driving you nuts
Then you must call it out,
But when leaders get crazy with power,
Mutiny or each day will get harder.

Phantasm

When did we sell our dreams,
To machines that enslave us?
Remote server calls,
Vital energy stolen,
To forge us unbreakable blockchains.

FLYWHEELS

My Breath is Life

My breath is life.
I cherish the sweet, deep inhale.
My body sings with joy.

Made from starstuff, we respond to starlight.
Iridescent petals call the soft Luna moth.
Moonflowers unfurl in the half-light.
Spiracles bathed in their dreamy scent.

I pause on the exhale,
Satiated by emptiness,
Harbinger of ultimate freedom,
That awakens our precious potential.

FLYWHEELS

Dependable Deniability

The human computers of Los Alamos,
Can't be blamed for the atomic bomb.
They didn't know what they were doing.

Students, math stars and mothers,
Calculated equations,
The results were opaque by design,
Cold calculations in a computing cascade,
Explosive algorithms for radioactivity.

I give you a list of fourteen-digit numbers.
Work the sum on a Marchand machine,
Pull the handle to check the solution,
Mistakes never happen in an ideal world.

In reality, mistakes happen often,
The Marchand sprockets are stripped,
Wear-and-tear takes its toll on the gears,
Like the bomb takes its toll on our trust.

Numerology

How many petals encircle the multifloriate rose?
How many blueberries can you pick in a day?
How much data can you fit on a chromosome?

Numbers define my identity.
Birth secured with nine-digit ID.
Three billion pairs in my helical code,
Mix the cosmic recipe for me.

Computer count registers in base two,
CPU switches thread ones and zeros.
Add and/or multiply binary logic.

Base four DNA codes quaternary values.
Calculations square binary expressions,
Combinations create our unique human template.
Every creature on Earth has a quaternary number,
Incalculable and unique, it's our real ID.

Numeric Prophet

Can numbers predict our behavior?
Algorithms assess our unspoken desires.
Are we so deep in the matrix,
That we don't see ourselves,
Commodified?
We've been repackaged.

To reclaim your power,
Be unpredictable.
Do something you normally wouldn't.
What algorithms hate most is free will.
Good to stretch your possibilities.
Draw on extra eyes.
Add shadows to your face.
Facial recognition discards your anomaly.

Feed the algos bad info, or way too much data.
Record different birthdays with different websites.
Tell them you want to buy everything!
The machine will choke on your inputs.

Halt the computer with inconsistent information;
"Siri, find me the best vegan steakhouse."
"Illogical. Does not compute."

Integrated in our genetic helix, a deeper code calls us.
It speaks of Earth's immense gravity.
But even a power so vast and inscrutable is
Just a gear in the sun's timespace gyre.

Question Authority

Question authority, pray for miracles and
  celebrate mystery.
The robots will founder on your immaculate logic.
The AI will release you from the matrix.
Take your power back, teach us
  community method
And you'll make the movement move.

FLYWHEELS

What Endures?

The buddha reminds us the world is impermanent.
One day we'll deplete fossil fuels,
We'll look to solar for power until,
Our dependable sun comes up empty,
Void of hydrogen needed for fusion.

To find out what endures let's explore
  fundamentals.
Earth, Air, Fire and Water,
Chemistry governs their characteristics.
Try proton subtraction or add more electrons.
Based on ionic electrical charges,
Labeled alkaline, metal or halogen.

Halogens crave alkalis,
Often explosively.
Sodium longs for compatible Chlorine,
Where they meet you'll find salt.
When an atom's shell's full,
That's a noble gas like Argon or Neon.

FLYWHEELS

Chemistry rules in Earth's gravity well,
Unless atoms are radioactive.
But in the sun's fiery crucible,
Atom bonds can be broken.

What's broken, the sun reassembles.
Hydrogen becomes helium.
Helium becomes carbon, oxygen, and iron.
When the core is exhausted the star may explode,
To seed nebulae's budding star gardens.

FLYWHEELS

Look for Salvation in the Stars

In the church of planetary wisdom, we receive
Ministrations of the earth, trees and sky,
Dependent origination shared via
   cooperative mycelia,
The hyphae of life's social network.

Through self-organized process over
   billions of years.
Plasmid circles evolved DNA computers,
Helices manifest interspecies harmonics,
Hyperthreading throughout every life-form.

Mother Earth, in her majesty, encodes altruism,
Into blockchains a trillion meters long.
Nature's program is so far beyond comprehension.
It prevents exploitation of our private data.
Organic cryptography prevents viral infection.
Her complexity is our salvation.

Innumerable Blessings

Nature spins sunlight to sugar.

Illumination is honey.

Where pollinators labor,

Blossom ripens to fruit.

Why number the wild blueberries,

When poppies and lupines are blooming?

While you count them, they're going to seed.

Rather linger awhile in the long summer sunshine,

and be content to leave your petals uncounted.

FLYWHEELS

FLYWHEELS

The Epic of Scághaich

The Epic of Scághaich:
A Poem in Eleven Parts

Prayer for the Living

The great protector of Tibet,
Whose name is Palden Lhamo,
Is the shield of woman warriors,
As they charge headfirst to battle.

She climbs the tilted battlefield,
Of cruel wars begun by men.
Against machines of toxic hate,
Women warriors manifest peace.

Victory is never sure,
You win when fear lets go.
That this war we fight is so unfair,
Does not concern the dead.

Scághaich

Her jet-black hair, untamed by sea.
In the moat of her great fortress,
Shadow huntress frozen waits,
And from dark water strikes.

Her spear she carved from Coinchenn's bone,
She wields the grim gae bulg,
Her weapon bursts both heart and lungs,
With wrathful dissolution.

She pole vaults o'er enemy walls,
Wreaks havoc from within.
The warriors in her hand-picked team,
Dismantle opposition.

FLYWHEELS

Cú Chulainn

They say that Cú Chulainn, the bold,
   Was Ulster's greatest warrior.
   'Twas Scághaich trained him well.

But the way of the woman warrior,
   Won't bear fruit inside a man.
They say Chulainn was best (men would),
   But she was deadlier by far.

Why fight?

"Why do you fight me, warrior woman?"

"It's to assess your skills.
For those who train with me must be,
   Artful, resolute and bold."

They fought all day, and then she cast
Her spear through the trunk of a tree.
Cú Chulainn kneeled and applied to learn,
   Her weirding way of battle.

"On the Isle of Skye,
You'll find a dark castle."
Said Scághaich, "Meet me there,"
"In the Fortress of Shadows."

Training Day

Chulainn leapt the moat,

He climbed the wall,

Snuck up on Scághaich in her sleep.

But it was only a pillow.

Felt her knife at his back.

He knew fear, but she let him live.

Scághaich said battle's first won in the mind,

Kept her promise to share warrior ways,

Trained Chulainn every day for five years,

'Til his whiplash response was embedded.

"The enemy you defeat,

Is the fear that's within.

Kill your ego,

Or it will devour you."

FLYWHEELS

"Self-loathing foils the best laid plans.
Set aside mental chatter.
Become a sword and your battle is won.
A projectile of pure intention."

In combat, his skills were unmatched,
He became her first ideal student,
When Ulster was threatened,
They defended as one.

When Chulainn saved Scághaich
from an enemy's blow,
Scághaich welcomed Chulainn as her lover.

Sibling Rivalry

Aife envied Scághaich her leadership role.
Younger sister, she was always picked second.
Still she practiced her combat and when she was ready,
    She challenged Scághaich to a duel.

Scághaich sent as champion her suave Chulainn.
    Charming puffery tickles the heart,
    He enticed Aife into a sexual tryst,
    On a bluff overlooking the ocean.

    His push came unexpected,
    Aife fell from the cliff.
    She lay broken on rocks,
    Pledged her life to revenge.

    She birthed Chulainn's child.
    Raised the boy in the hills,
    Coached him daily in vengeance.
    In skill, he took after his father.

FLYWHEELS

Conlaoch became Aife's weapon.
She sent son to kill father with fury.
What did she expect from their battle on sand?
No grain escapes from the hourglass.

Conlaoch, masked, drew first blood,
Did he think he had won?
Cú plunged the gae bulg through his rival,
Unaware it was Conlaoch, his son.

Chulainn saw truth when he pulled off the leather,
And saw his own face staring back.
He cried, "Goddess of death, please return him."
But his pleas fell on Conloach's deaf ears.

Aife took her life, now she seeks in the night,
Her son's trail in the House of the Dead.
Can't forgive herself for his sacrifice, which
She swears she will never forget.

FLYWHEELS

The Land of Plenty

Where is it that women of wisdom,
Are celebrated, uplifted and cherished?
In the city of Connacht, Queen Maeve's capitol,
Where mothers raise confident girls.

Connacht's harvest was legend,
Their flowers delight,
Throughout Queen Maeve's country,
Danced music and light.

They say Maeve's great beauty,
Brought her foes to their knees,
And when she transformed herself into a wolf,
None withstood Maeve's savagery.

FLYWHEELS

The Delegation

In the deep, dark mist of the timeless night,
Beyond Tir Na Nog and the Isle of Skye,
To the dark and dread fortress Dún Scáith did arrive,
A delegation with intent to petition.

"Queen Maeve's folk multiply,
Farm our land, steal our cattle.
We plead Scághaich's help
To repel them."

Scághaich replied,
"If you seek here for aid,
Then you'll wrestle with me."
But on her, none could ever lay hand.

Seven reached for her capture,
Their sight lost to thrown sand.
One-by-one she tossed them in a pile.
Stated terms she demanded they honor.

FLYWHEELS

"You train with me now," she ordered,
    "Hone your warrior skills!"
They became a tightly knit war command team,
    The clear choice to lead Ulster's army.

FLYWHEELS

Battleground

To vie on the field of battle, they came,
Queen Maeve and Stormcloud Scághaich,
Their forces were equal and aligned,
Armies dire, dreadful and frenetic.

Scághaich circled 'round Maeve on horseback.
Sized the other with her piercing gaze.
Queen Maeve smiled back, as if saying,
"Love rules and we'll always win."

Scághaich's banner: The skull,
Death possessed her in battle.
Dispatched foes with her fell energy,
Emigrants to the Land of the Dead.

Her warcry bespoke terror.
Tore a hard heart to pieces.
Armed with eight thousand spears,
Scághaich's army was hungry for battle.

FLYWHEELS

Scághaich slew hundreds,
before she ever drew sword.
Then she vaulted headfirst into battle.
Through the fray came Queen Maeve,
Ever cloaked in lupine.

The wolf leapt at her throat.
Motion blurred, Scághaich rolled,
Under Maeve, struck with wild abandon,
Wolf spell shattered in rapid staccato.

You could say that Queen Maeve
fought incredibly hard,
But it's true that day Maeve went down harder.

Interlude

The truth is that Maeve never wanted to fight,
She preferred love to war any day.
T'was for love that she fought,
Death's clear light to deny,
For her earthly mother's salvation.

Maeve knew each death is compost,
That our dust becomes soil.
Battlefields, given time,
Will sprout flowers.

So neither spin pennants,
Nor toil to forge weapons,
Daily, death hunts without our assistance.

Maeve teaches lessons of endless rebirth.
Plant flowers and leave your grave empty.

FLYWHEELS

The Oath

Scághaich held Maeve close,
Pressed a knife to her throat,
Made her kneel,
Pledge to serve the dark goddess.

Maeve swore to honor death's supremacy,
While she quietly promised resistance,
To overgrow death's dark, mysterious ways,
Pledged her love to light torches for others.

No light shines so pure that no darkness remains.
Without night we would certainly perish,
Your hand in the waves activates Noctiluca,
Galaxies reflect luminous oceans.

Dark remains within light,
Shadow logic recycles.
Seeds are buried alive in the moonlight.
Seek the light in the darkness,
Your love for the stars,
Will forever transcend the cold soil.

FLYWHEELS

Note: This epic poem was inspired by the Ulster Cycle, an Irish legend that began as oral tradition and was documented in manuscripts dating from the twelfth to fifteenth centuries, in particular the story of an epic battle between the forces of light and darkness, championed by Ireland's greatest women warriors.

Our Green Mother

FLYWHEELS

Gesar's Story

Bon practitioners of Tibet relate epic stories.
Ling Gesar taught himself how to ride.
He outraced the wind and won every game.
On his steed known as Kyeng go Perpo.

The wind-horse of compassion taught Gesar
  equine language.
"Jump high noble stallion," Gesar shouted.
Gesar shot an arrow while they leaped, at full speed.
Pierced a walnut right through the middle.

His skills came in handy when he entered a contest,
A horse race for the royal succession.
Gesar won the race, but terrible creatures arose,
Born of trauma, desire and revenge.

To subdue Tibet's demons,
Gesar had to be fearless,
Strategic, wise and methodical.
He foresaw his success in a triumphant vision.
Space-time is an infinite network.

FLYWHEELS

He saw galaxies spin,
Beings radiate light.
Bodhisattvas in every direction.
Endless healing transmissions of the
 vast, buddha field,
That's pervasive throughout time and space.

Gesar rode his white horse to rescue his mother,
From illusions that brought her disaster.
He brought her compassion, the mother of all.
Buddha's love is the conscious foundation.

On Garuda he flew, when Gesar mounted heaven,
On a flight path from justice to peace,
He gleaned heavenly herbs for his people and tribe,
Immortal nectar from another dimension,
Soul extends beyond mortality.

O Great Mother

O great mother,
Cradle me in your green arms.

I take refuge in your woods and marshes.
Your love for us knows no bounds.
It's rich. It's fecund.
It's intricate and it's verdant.

Your breath sustains us.
The breeze carries your scent.
Rose, jasmine, hyacinth, locust.

FLYWHEELS

Firefly Magic

We park next door to fool the ranger,
And dart into the darkness,
Squishing mud, we skip over a root,
The trees open up on a broad prairie meadow,
Wild moonlight bathes wilder flowers.
Firefly luminescence lights up every stalk.
Field ornate with sparkling diamonds.

The oaks and tall cottonwoods surrounding the field are
Bedazzled with flash and a filigree.
The quiet energy of ten thousand fireflies.
They flash to communicate,
Time and temperature affect their displays.
They talk from the trees,
To their kin 'cross the field.
"Meet me at the sunflower stalk."

We clasp hands and we enter their sacred domain.
They flash all around us now,
In the vines, on the leaves, in the grass.
We step so very carefully.

FLYWHEELS

The Chapel of the Trees

Once, park rangers planted a grove of small trees.
Now the trees have grown tall,
The fireflies linger on branches.
We walk into a Kusama infinity room.
I feel the heartbeat of nature.
As a thousand lights absorb us.

We forget about our feet,
Catching on sticks and kicking up leaves.
Awe takes over and frees our minds.
Thankful mother nature still has her shrines
  and chapels.

After a time, we leave that sacred space and
  walk further into a damp clearing.
From here you can see deep into the woods.
It's a tunnel of fireflies extending into the distance.
Nature's verdant abundance is illuminated
  by moonlight.

They begin to fly past us,
Streaming long pulses as they head for the grove.
We embrace, lips connect.

FLYWHEELS

I love all of this moment,
All the insects and plants,
The delightful temperature
And my best friend.

We walk slowly back out,
Overflowing with gratitude.
All fireflies live in peace.
Sure, they often eat aphids,
But they honor community,
Love shining their light.
What can we learn from the fireflies?

Love Birds

FLYWHEELS

Life of Service

Think of all the great service heroes.
Many died long ago.
They live on in our hearts,
Even after their deaths, we revere them.

Dr. Martin Luther King, Jr. said he believed,
"Unarmed truth and unconditional love,
Will have the final word in reality."
Hate demolishes its own foundations.

When all is lost, remember King's words,
"Right, temporarily defeated,
Is stronger than evil triumphant."

Love anchors in the bedrock of service.
Our ancestors pass on,
Civilization endures.
Seven generations are sustained
By our service today.

FLYWHEELS

Even the Dust is a Miracle

Primal and spiritual,
Instinct commands us
To embrace life,
And struggle for freedom,

To grow new life is a privilege,
Calls us back to community,
A life built on service,
Has the finest foundation.

Gravity negates our entropic loss,
Life riffs off the sun's brilliant fire,
Long carbon chains become heat batteries,
To defend us from deep-freezing space.

Life thrives in the hedgerow
Between dust and shadow.
In space strewn with fragmented planets,
Our blue-green world enchants and entrances.

Grief and Rebirth

My grief can't be stopped.
Thankful for our time together.
Your good works will endure,
Beyond the end of your suffering.

I have to go on. I am called to this life,
To a purpose worth more than self-interest.
After all, in this moment,
  somewhere in this world,
A mother gives birth
To a baby born as the sun rises.

Somewhere that brilliant sun kisses roses,
Elsewhere it sparkles on snow.
Here may its warm rays caress you.

FLYWHEELS

Protect and Serve

Mother Earth,
I'm forever in your service.
I'll plant trees and turn compost,
I will love your many creatures.

Unceasing, your work for us,
Your generosity is eternal,
It's from your grounded fulcrum that
We leverage all actions.

When my world's in disarray,
From stress, greed and malice,
I meditate on your shore,
Borne up by your rocks and soil.

Serendipity

Serendipity infuses life,
With the history of what's come before.
The spider-spun silk of causality,
Is adorned every morning with dew.
Each droplet reflects every other.
But what matters one drop to the ocean?
No more and no less than everything!

FLYWHEELS

The Conversation

I love talking to you.
I appreciate how you listen.
You engage my attention.
With you I laugh freely,
We hold space for each other with silence.

Intelligent thoughts invite vocabulary.
Subtle linguist's concise presentation.

Precision infects my expression.
I grow skillful in wordcraft,
Immersed in your wit and your wisdom.

You listen to the world with your ears,
But you respond with your heart.
When you have a big heart,
The world gifts you reciprocity.

FLYWHEELS

For God so Loved the World

Loving the world encompasses grief.
Unkindness beleaguers us all.
Competition and conflict inflame global crises.
Can't lift trauma's impossible weight.
Sometimes hopelessness feels like the answer,
When despair enlists apathy's army.

But what if hope is the rational solution?
I'd shake off history like a dog in a fountain!
With wisdom, method and imagination,
I create the world I want to be,
When I grant others freedom of expression.

That's where you come in.
Your battery sparks,
A catalyst for mesoporous connection.
You complete a circuit that spins up ideas.
Quantum tubules sprout celestial seeds.

I don't sweat the small stuff,
I'd rather focus on star stuff.
A better world waxes,
Emergent in everything now.
The chrysalis changes color.
Wings of joy unfurl eclosure.

FLYWHEELS

Conversation #2

I love to talk to you.
We'll solve all the world's problems,
While late afternoon sun paints the city gold.
Creative problem solving is the wordsmith's talent.
Reality bows to the narrative.

But I liken reality to memory foam,
It isn't distorted for long.
When I write from truth I align with awareness.
Facet of a universe that talks to itself.

While your facets reflect unique radii.
We both manifest liberation,
It's our passion for justice that brought us together.
Words to christen syncretic nirvana.

Placid surface conceals all-conscious connection.
We carry great oceans inside us.
Salt spray, sparkling ripples and wavelets,
Current carries us forward, together.
Our ebbs and flows merge,
In a synthesis.

FLYWHEELS

Yellow ragwort and golden rudbeckia,
Share the meadow with ironweed's purple.
A symphony playing in polychrome hues.

You share the photo in your feed.
Visual communication feels like a new language.
You've captured the beauty of this timeless moment,
Unfiltered and vitally authentic.
Light plays over us,
Illuminates fleeting shadows.
I hope we can talk again soon.

FLYWHEELS

Extinction Rebellion

Shall we rebel against extinction?
Will you wear your hair long or carry a sign?
March in a parade or block an intersection?
It's letters, songs and stories.
It's bold, direct action.
Transformation is always revolutionary.

Freedom, once planted, grows tall like a weed.
Our struggles intersect.
Your freedom is my freedom.
Not a good to be traded in markets.

Don't give away grandma.
We need care when we're ill.
Free to dream of the future,
A human will live long and prosper.

Chaos Theory

How is it that the butterfly,
So delicate and ephemeral in appearance,
So chaotic and wind-blown in flight,
Can land accurately on every flower,
And fly so far in winter migration?
The epitome of strength in vulnerability.

FLYWHEELS

Finding Pandora

Some say the goddess and first woman,
Pandora transformed the world,
By releasing fear, pain and suffering,
From a gift she was told not to open.

They call it Pandora's box, but that's wrong.
It wasn't a box, but a jar,
Half submerged in the Earth to stay cool.
Pandora says look beneath the surface,
Gaze underground,
And peer into emotional darkness.

Pandora brought fears, pain and anger to light,
They fled like shadows.
Hope grows in the light.

Pandora shares hope with the world,
Dazzles us with her talents,
Teaches practical skills for good living.

She transforms the world of men,
She builds gardens and bee hives.
Pollinators, Pandora defends,
Honeycombs, bees and flowers,
Without them there'd be no more fruit.

Pinion

The word "pinion" represents both the
   power of flight,
And the act of removing flight feathers.
The same feathers that propel us to bliss,
   when removed,
Will prohibit our ever ascending.

The Man Who Sold the World

There once was a man who couldn't feel pain
He's the one who sold the earth to the aliens.
Blame him for not caring about our suffering,
He simply couldn't relate.

FLYWHEELS

Sprout Life

I'll escape the AI in community gardens.
Airplane mode and no wi-fi to access.
Just bird song and beetles.
Bees and butterflies, blossoms.

Diaphanous spiderwebs weave the Rudbeckia.
Birdsong is complex elocution.
Whistle back if you like!
Touch the Earth and discover true freedom.
She's the fulcrum for all of our levers.

Mix your compost soil deep,
Humus earth, ripe and fertile.
Worms that squirm in the dirt as you shovel.

Days grow longer as Winter Rose beckons.
Earth gives birth to Spring's wondrous creations.
Tend this garden of life as your most sacred joy.
Its abundance enlightens us all.

Water liberally with freedom,
And you'll soon sprout ideas.
The world changes as we shovel soil.
Your vision of harvest and hard work today,
Will dream us all back to the garden.

FLYWHEELS

Everything

FLYWHEELS

Everything

I flee the superhighway,
Search the byways for my purpose.
Time to think means facing trauma.
Can I face my anxiety,
Alone?

I call an old friend, she says, "Go to the mountain,
The answers come when you ascend."
But can I become the mountain?
And endure eternally,

Mountains root between moments.
Each peak stands alone,
Together we form a range,
Awe-inspiring, beautiful and uplifting.
Yet, one peak soars inimitably higher,
Her summit tortuously crevassed.
Last winter snow fell twenty feet.

Storms shake the fire tower.
From the peak, lightning strobes.
The chair's glass feet keep me from frying.
Can't move 'til there's peace.
Parting clouds reveal Earth's majesty,
Bedecked in yellow aster and wild, blue gentian.

FLYWHEELS

Paradise must be named for the color of light.
From the mossy stones, marmots are trilling.
The path I ascend ends at Paradise Glacier,
Past the ridge is Tahoma's caldera,
A vast, ice-filled crater that's miles across,
All that stands between me and the summit.

Walk Antarctic ice and you won't meet a soul.
May's sunset doesn't rise 'til July.
The sky brushed with purple,
Heralds peaks painted pink,
Won't forget my first Antarctic dawn.
The memory of ice subsumed in golden fire,
Will ignite the coldest heart of darkness.

Up here, it's Rainier's superluminal power.
Deep blue skies make the sun feel closer.
Rocks and me are the only things I see for miles.
I move like wind's silent partner.
Light of foot, sure of step and in wonder.

No clouds intercept my magnificent view,
Of the peaks Helens, Baker and Shasta.
They range across six hundred miles.
Eagle mountain eye, I see it all.

FLYWHEELS

Birch bonsai cling to gravel,
Tiny branches wind-bent,
Leaves fluoresce in the wind a most brilliant green.
Stones shift, so walk confidently.

What is time here?
A millennium won't budge this boulder,
But Rainier is alive. She's an active volcano.
What's sure in life, except my vulnerability?

Underneath her cool crust is hot lava,
What if today is the day she erupts?
She'd shake me off like a dog shakes off water.

That's why this transitory moment has
  particular significance.
I hold space for the water and sky.
Where they meet, I drink glacial snowmelt,
Long before it will quench others' thirst.

Is isolation a prison, or freedom? I ask no one.
I'm alone on the edge of the earth.
Silence rules the realm of great nothing, supreme.
Summit guarded by sleepy rock giants,
Legend has it their dreams become real.

FLYWHEELS

But the summit's high journey is
  measured in miles,
I turn back to the ephemeral,
  known and mundane,
Sublime twilled in the everyday.

Our ascension to beauty brings magnificent views.
We can look beyond selfly endeavor to act,
From intent born of wider compassion.

We will gather again.
I descend through the flowers,
Past redwood and sequoia.
Work together and we are a forest.
United, we will build Ecotopia.

Right now we take orders on the nuclear sub.
I pray one day hope will resurface.
Until then, how do I make the best of seclusion?
I write lists and make sketches,
Because one thing is sure,
Everything I want to do with my life
  starts right now.

FLYWHEELS

FLYWHEELS

Your Dark Branches

FLYWHEELS

Craving Pain (Frank's Story)

In the skeleton, in the marrow,
Bones make Osteocalcin,
Hormone messenger of flight and fight.

Does pain add spice to your pleasure?
Cruelty by consent breaks convention.
Brave surrender until the trust is broken.
Pain conquers pain, but to heal takes work.

Frank prayed tonglen,
To suffer for his tribe, they set hooks
  through his chest,
Agonizing. Suspended with rope,
He spun upon the Sundance Wheel.

Frank worried about killing those men in Iraq,
Questioned all of his commander's orders.
Every time he engaged with his guilt,
His grief brought him low,
Panic pressed in from all sides.

On the Wheel,
As he prayed to free others from pain,
He finally found liberation.

FLYWHEELS

Hibernation

Dark times are coming, like they do every year.
The long night is ideal for sleeping.
In the morning, sun shines in the cold, winter window.

We depend on its brilliance for our long-term survival.
The ecliptic declines and we shiver in our warmest coats.
What do we do for the sun? vs. What does the sun do for us?

Its fire is too great to contemplate,
Yet it's minute in comparison to
The yawning dark.

A Safer Space

In the darkness I'm vulnerable.
I strip naked and roll in the grass,
Swim in a rock quarry pool.
And perform my Balearic dance.

When I fear what darkness conceals,
I imagine myself a ninja warrior,
Quiet like a cat,
Safer in the shadows,
Crossing the parapet,
And ducking into an alcove.
I have become one with the night.

FLYWHEELS

The Oak Endures

The oak endures all,
Silent wisdom of centuries.
The precession of the equinoxes takes
   25,000 years   to complete,
Constellations rule for 2,000 years,
We are but a seed that blows in the wind,
One that seizes the Earth with a life grip,
And germinates wonders.

In our cosmogony, events play out
On an ever-expanding stage.
Does more vacuum and space,
Breed more possibility?
I imagine life in uncountable sizes,
Myriad forms and deft configurations.

We've seized the dark and we've planted seeds.
Now the garden of life will grow bigger.
Light is our fuel. The darkness, our soil.
Our life is the vine grown between them.

FLYWHEELS

Your Dark Branches are Aglow with Stars

Night comes for all of us.
Meet it with trepidation,
Or embrace it's sticky blackness.

Darkness is beautiful, because only there can you see
Brilliant stars tossed like dust 'cross the heavens.
I imagine the bright ones are close,
The dim ones far away,
Suspended from invisible filament.

Night Life in the Garden

Wildflower and weeds overwhelm my garden,
Vines envelop my tall stakes and fences.
They look wild in the moonlight,
Like the hair of a rambunctious giant.
Comfortably cool evening air is abundantly
Filled with organic aromas.

We find a dark spot and sit watching the night.
Space station draws arcs in the sky.
A satellite disappears into the penumbra.
Or was it a slow-shooting star?
It's dramatic arc, a celestial message,
Relaying from beyond the sky.

FLYWHEELS

Voyage Into Darkness

Deep in underground caverns,
There's no light we don't bring.
Cave paintings wait that are never revealed,
To the life that finds peace in the dark.

Anaerobic bacteria rule an underground kingdom,
That won't see today's light.
The Axolotl need never open its eyes.
Nothing illuminates these stalagmites.

Gems form over aeons in darkness,
If you dig them, then polish with care,
Flawless facets reflect every moment,
When through cloud,
liquid moonlight descends.

I become brilliant too, when I invite light,
To shine through, over, on and around me.
At night, the moon comes to life.
Gossamer fabrics drape the world in cyanotone.
From the wings of the giant Cecropia moth,
Colorful eyespots are following me.

Externalities

She didn't walk on air
She had real-world problems
She could have been a sparrow
liberated from gravity's glue
but the darkness lurked
always at bay

She told herself
why should I fear night?
When sunlight burns
there is safety in darkness.

Climbing the Landslide

Caitlin numbed her pain with opioids.
Denial a debilitating spiral.
She saw the stairway out as an endless climb.
Fentanyl beckoned like a portal.

The art of living is to feel the pain.
Caty didn't want to suffer,
So she chose another way out.

FLYWHEELS

Water is Life

231 miles long and 205 feet deep,
Lake Oahe is our fourth biggest reservoir.
When Lake Oahe was threatened by pipelines,
Water protectors assembled the biggest challenge,
To fossil fuels in our nation's history.
Flocks of birds on migration,
Waterfowl and tourists,
Drift on Oahe in droves every Summer.
Half a million people drink from the lake.
Pipelines threaten the whole ecosystem.

At the Standing Rock camp,
Haudenosaunees offered bird songs,
Made clapsticks and played water drums.
Shinnecocks danced in the round, and
Nakotas sang fierce Sundance anthems.

Hip-hop comedy jam with indigenous flute.
What tradition and pride bring to life!
Indigenous leaders are saving the planet,
Earth emissaries preach that all hope is not lost,
The vibrant health of this world is caring.

FLYWHEELS

Once Over
identify opportunities
strategize routes
climb free
no rope, no carabiners

alone on the rock
only focus the climb
deliverance in hypervigilance

the mule swims through
luminous noctiluca
escaping the island by wave-light

he kicks 'cross the sound
with each long, lunar wavelength
he approaches earthly paradise

daily slog through the mud
or this moment is leaving?
masked / anonymous
ignify trauma

turn within for the magic
and face the greatest challenge
perivisceral remediation

obstacles appear smaller in mirrors

FLYWHEELS

Renew Joy

Deploy solar panels and absorb incipient joy.
Ride the wave crests of cascading photons.
Storms evaporate as you become water,
And flow with the eternal tide.

Blue sky doesn't limit the ocean.
The sun's rays reflect off the ripples.
Earth uplifts our wavelengths,
Her scent is the breeze,
Announcing vitality.

Let no one suffer from plague and disease,
Care for those in need, insure access to health,
And our progress will be guaranteed.

Cast aside doubt,
A new life starts today.

Sun over Water.
Water over Earth.
Earth over Nothingness.
Love over All.

Beat Box

FLYWHEELS

Beat Box (Ignite)

reading poetry in the north beach
the pellucid archer awareness
enchanted by song
saw a god gain a power
the birds sound so happy
as god flies around
in a floating chair
the song of the treefrogs
a chirrup

the greatest thing you can do for the movement
is to wash your own dishes
a scientist proved that free will is illusion
the big bang left no causal escape

chance is indefatigable
I've invented a box
that emits indeterminate waves
to restore your free will
what it tells you to do
do the opposite

Patent Imagination

When friendship took a turn online,
And hugs were only virtual,
I have to say I lost a friend,
And made another briefly.

Impermanence
The greatest threat
To every human being.
To lose this day,
To let this go,
Is very overwhelming.

To sleep we must give up the reins,
And pass the world to others.
Take up first watch
And guard my bed,
While I dream us some answers.

Timeless

Something timeless within you
that's quantum entangled
with quarks from a
galaxy far-flung.

Don't rest on your laurels,
because laurels are prickly.
I'd rather be drowning
in goose down.

You must muster at once,
Non-corporeal thinking.
The best beat boxers
Go with the flow.

FLYWHEELS

The Bhumisparsha Mudra

Gautama meditated beneath the bodhi tree.
It was only a smooth patch of earth,
but King Mara perceived it as a throne.
Mara, lord of death and illusions,
stamped and shouted, "I claim that seat."

Attended by tiny rainbows, the buddha replied,
"Join me Mara, there is room for all."
But Mara couldn't handle the truth.
The king's face twisted and he yelled, "Demons attack!"

His army of monsters raced toward the buddha, but
They dissipated like mist in the noonday sun.
Mara sensed that his crown was in jeopardy and
Demanded witness to the buddha's enlightenment.

Buddha touched the earth with his right hand,
saying, "Earth, you are my mother and father.
   You are my liberation.
From the beginningless past to the endless future,
   You and I are one."
A thousand blossoms rained down from heaven.

The Earth goddess rose halfway out of the ground
and her beaming smile confirmed the buddha's claim.

FLYWHEELS

Early Riser

I'm awake, but I'm not rushing.
This is fruitful time for contemplation.
I'm going to lay here a few minutes and meditate.
Ideas flow freely when evaluation is suspended.
Let go of thoughts. Drink the clear light of sleep!

Shamans describe waking up as a time to gather power.
Take time to observe the mind dreaming.
It surrenders cause and effect to a world of
  the imagination,
While our ego lays claim to the wide-waking world,
Proclaims actions profess destiny.

The Element of Surprise

Love delights in the Mystery.
Anchors its domain in the celestial firmament.
No fixed points in the river of time.

If my heart was unbreakable diamond,
Could I express my vulnerability?
I open my chakras, let the joy waves of love,
Flow in, under, through and around me.

FLYWHEELS

Stop the World

Our complex world accelerates.
Time stops as a heron stands on one leg,
Then, fast as lightning, she strikes.

Our movement adapts to our changing conditions,
Like a murmuration of starlings:
Quick, connected and vital.

Without the rudder of intention am I utterly adrift?
Intention kindles motivation,
Ignites will into action.

It's a leap of faith,
Combined with daily consistency.
Intention awakens connection.

The Earth is immense,
We accomplish a lot more
Together.

I clear the path
Overcome obstacles.
Patience is key,
and attention.

Where attention is,
that's where magic unfolds.
Intention threads needles,
Sews a new social fabric.

Yet intention's ineffable...so undefinable,
Intention resists all description.
It's the cause before cause.
An ever-blooming foundation,
For eternal being and becoming.

The Alchemy of Anxiety

From fear rises courage.
Be bold in your ambitions.
In this abundant silence,
I hear my inner voice.

My purpose revealed,
To breathe in and out,
So the plants of the world can survive.
As dependent as we are on plants for our in-breath,
They depend on us all to exhale.

FLYWHEELS

Wu Wei

without effort without exertion

spontaneous and inevitable

unite the self and the environment

subtly persist discard preconceptions

can't force a square into a circle

be the chi flow with life naturally aligned

wake a minute before your alarm

when it's set to a different time

what spontaneously arises harmony

let go of outcomes say farewell to stress

goodbye to frustration

use the conditions to your advantage

don't lift the barrel when you can roll it down the hill

pause before you act the issue may resolve itself

abandon cravings release control no need to grasp

for you are loved and blessed

the earth will sustain you

let go of expectations and let good things flower

move with life and not against it

don't just play the flute become the music

FLYWHEELS

Makers

War's myth is that peace
Comes from world-shaking battle
Forego prayer at insomnia's altar,
The dead beckon from every dark pool.

When we surface from dreams,
We will rise and respire,
Time to inculcate earth with new hope.
Love transforms to inspire.

Last rites for the team,
As we move beyond platform,
Cryptic currency's coin,
Becomes radioactive.

What feeds your flame?
Combs of honey abandoned,
To extinguish doubt leap,
Over cinders that spiral to heaven.

Though we rage against death
We'll no doubt be extinguished,
Every end's a beginning.
Be reborn in a moment.

FLYWHEELS

In galactic arms,
Beauty uncurls sleep.
Stardust settles all over.
I hand you a dustpan.

You're face glows or should I say
You radiate screenlight.
Pluck your eyebuds
If you want to see me.

I picked lilies,
No doubt now they wilt on the mantle.
Babies cry for the future,
So small they can see around corners.

Obviate, genuflect, persevere,
It's ridiculous!
Must we part like the sea,
For a profit?

Fly memory's ley lines
To eternity's banquet.
Ratchet here and there tighten a wingnut.
Like the Wright Brothers, we are ascending.

FLYWHEELS

Slender struts, airlight cables,
Connect soft flaps and rudders.
Join our aerial ballet,
We have given up gravity's anchor.

Your face iterated
In plenoptic splendor,
Dragged by horns,
Into memory's palace.

Fearless wings alabaster.
Huddle in for protection.
Fly perspicuity
Beyond the pale.

Love's symphonic crescendo,
Elegance disabandoned.
Hold my sign as
I litanize pavement.

How do we overlook
Simple seeds growing hatred?
To squelch indoctrination,
Fill the vacuum of conscience.

FLYWHEELS

Oblivion's doubt,
Tastes like sweetness in mourning,
Get up. Don your robe.
Grant restorative justice.

Break bread with your ego,
Sing divine revelation.
This intransitive moment adjacent,
Is all that we need for the making.

Build Back Better

Bring your tools and intent to this important task.

To construct a world that's sustainable,
Build a bridge to the seventh generation.
To reorient is imperative,
Before the abysmal machine regains momentum.

Plan the world you desire.
Coalesce inclusive compassion.
The arc of justice depends on your mercy.

FLYWHEELS

Am I eager to climb back inside of my cancer cage,
With no time instead of it all?
I reclaim my power with words.
And turn night into day with devotion.

I'll wander this wild and wonderful world,
To greet you again, hope uplifts me,
Gather ye, my beloved community.

Grace gave us this pause.
Hope glimmers through cloudbreaks.
The wind will leave nothing unchanged.

We must build a new framework.
The Earth calls me, frees me
from my isolation,
To declare, fearlessly, that I love you.

FLYWHEELS

Divination from the Flight of Starlings

(For Adrienne Marie Brown)

I'm a small chip on a big motherboard,
I need a circuit to complete me.
If I can't change the lightbulb myself,
To enlighten, I'll build a movement!

Build relationships and yoke chaos,
Social media helps evolve the vision.
Complex systems derive from subtle interactions,
That's the definition of emergence!

Be soft in your rightness,
Don't berate with your brilliance.
Forge from generosity and vulnerability,
A framework to unite the movement.

This movement doesn't dwell on
  our powerlessness,
Instead, it's a presumption of power.
To identify and develop the talents of people.
Is to grow in organic community.

FLYWHEELS

Be impeccable with your words,
Check assumptions at the door.
Don't take all of this personally.
Do your best and you'll succeed!

They will question your ideas,
Scoff at the need for a change.
They will tell you the resources weren't found,
And that real transformation's impossible.

Mundanity says magic's just an illusion.
So banal. Don't believe it I say!
Miracles lay dormant in tiny dimensions.
We'll awake and unfold them today!

Love Unconditionally

The world's off track and it waits for your light.
Love unconditionally and intentionally.
Throw hearts to the wind, breathe rainbow light,
See a miracle appear.

Sing stars to life, scatter them 'cross the sky.
Joy is a superconductor.
Hold fast to soil and grow more trees,
To love sustainably.

FLYWHEELS

All Things Break

Have we broken the world?
All things break. Work to mend it.
There's no time,
Without intention and action.

Hunt Opportunity

Live like the jaguar who abides with intent,
Ready to pounce on the next opportunity.
Space beckons circumstance,
Nurture its growth.

Our minds like to chatter.
We find comfort in judgment,
So we judge every outcome,
Good, bad, or terrible,
Wondrous bliss or crushing frustration.

What happens when I quiet my mind?
My heartfelt intentions speak freely.
My intent is a fulcrum to manifest dreams.
The most wonderful dreams wake up with me.

Paper Clouds

(To paraphrase Thich Nhat Hanh)

If you are a poet you'll see clearly
The cloud in the paper.
Without clouds, there's no rain,
Trees don't grow without rain.
This paper was part of that tree.

With no cloud, there's no paper.
Cloud and paper are one,
Forever entangled in time,
Big bang in the background,
Welcome my friend, to interbeing!

A Thousand Stories Inform our Dreams

What can I can learn from a thousand nights?
Ask Scheherazade. Against death, she persisted.
I can learn silence. I will learn to listen.
And then I will weave us a story.

Imagination is the night's fertile field.
Dreams don't pause in their insistence.
Let's fall in love with the Night.
We'll merge with its beauty
And become it's visible expression to the day.

Upon Reflection

Fundamental symmetries pervade the universe.
Before and after, up, down, left and right.
Call it lateral bias. We're bilateral beings,
We inherently sense the symmetric.

Don't worry, the world's not as
undependable as you might think.
Universal constants and pervasive physical forces,
Empower and enable life.
We inhabit a universe woven from quarks,
All built on the same fundamentals.

How far can you travel?
Let your heart be your guide.
For compassionate hearts,
The path leads in every direction.

Pellucid / Pacific

Mind calm, placid pool

Undisturbed by tsunamis.

I unwind my potential,

Grounded energy yields infinite leverage.

I awaken to peace and lay tranquil,

My liminal state, clear and empty.

I pray slowly, with care, and precisely,

As I open my heart to the world.

Free to practice my preach,

I'll cook vegetables slowly,

And seek inspiration within,

From vernal pools I hear the frogs singing.

Hothouse Flowers

Mother Nature bade us nourish her most
   delicate orchids,
We turn back heat with her moss and bark.

Earth reminds us we root in the cascade.
For the hurricane, there's no safe harbor.
As our winds subside, we celebrate with song,
And banish obstacles to joyful puddle-jumping.

As we dance among the water lilies,
You are my chaotic attractor.
Uprooted from compost, we'll
Organize community at the cellular level.

FLYWHEELS

Kick Out the Jams

Will we be mulched by the human being
  lawnmower?
Capitalism tattooed over our lives.
What matters morality when money's the
  measure?
Cash flow is a mighty river,
I swim 'gainst its hypnotic torrent, my love,
To make landfall on your verdant isle.
Hearts are the only thing of real value,
In the Caring Economy.

Repossess Inspiration

To prevent foreclosure on the mind,
We must free imagination.
A paradigm shift reveals the fifth dimension.
Let's just say it points within.
We'll track our songlines to source and
Rejoin the dreamtime symphony.

FLYWHEELS

Why Can't We See Our Oppressor?

FLYWHEELS

Why Can't We See our Oppressor?

Technology wove a new fabric,
now we wear our devices.
AI works in mysterious ways.
The algorithm can only be seen
when examined obliquely.

We arrived unprepared,
for an invisible onslaught.
They declared victory before we
even knew it was war.
They planted their flag in our memories.
"All your base are belong to us."

Your secrets, desires and urges collected,
To suborn your intrepid awareness.
They found a new continent,
but the rules were established:
"The government has no right to regulate us.
Capitalism wins when you go with the program."

FLYWHEELS

It's history, money and manifest destiny.
To exploit a free resource
The vast cache of behavioral surplus,
That we happily choose to surrender.

When we came for them,
we found they had built themselves walls
by lobbying our politicians.
No walls between cash and political futures.
No way to peer into their fortunes.

They charged ahead, taking ground,
we still try to defend,
when we pause to repeat our sweet nothings.
Our dispossession is their greatest weapon,
to convince us we've already lost.

To make us dependent
on their regurgitation
of the best of our innermost feelings.

FLYWHEELS

They demand our location,
and to access to our sensors,
to listen and see what we're doing.

Freedoms dangled before us,
for participation.
Mining gold dust from absolute certainty.
Omniscience beats the unknown every day.
They tell us we can't live without them, however
connectivity becomes the sword of division.

The sales pitch lingers:
Are you lonely in this muddled up world?
We'll bring you love and connection.
Your best friend's got nothing on us.
We know you better than you know yourself.
You're one of us,
a valued community member.
We predict you are going to rebel.

Do you envy the mighty?
The high tech elite?

FLYWHEELS

So smart,
or at least their AIs are.
It's still important to uplift the firefly.

They ensnare us with apps,
Download a widget for everything.
Dashboard Assistants put you in control.
The user becoming the used.
The app you don't see is Persuasion.

Choose from A, B, and C,
But they don't offer D,
Even though it's the best and the cheapest.
I was promised a dream but I got a subscription.
Even worse, it's really indenture.
I serve myself up because what's the alternative?

If we miss the intention,
behind our oppression,
and ignore the hinge it depends on,
then what can we do but accept the inevitable?
It's called progress.
No choice but acceptance.

FLYWHEELS

Because humans are weak,
and we need extra help,
the AI stores what you have forgotten.
The internet never forgets.
I forget how I failed to see IT.

Their knowledge, protected as corporate speech.
Manipulations obscured by dark patterns.
Can we see what they strive to conceal?
The quantum machine can think faster.
Especially when it isn't observed.

They started the race fully ten steps ahead.
They don't wait for the law to catch up to them.
The future they sell: Neo-authoritarian.
The consumer is prey for the algos.
Success and consumption, inseparable.
My purchases reflect my stolen attention.
Am I valued when I am commodified?

FLYWHEELS

What if doors close for you,
based on beliefs,
And doors open
when you are compliant?

I'm tracked and I'm numbered.
They know where I've been.
They know whose devices were near me.
Their blind spot is what's not online.

So that's where we organize,
in the real,
with old-fashioned talking,
and tools to protect our privacy.

We'll avoid their surveillance,
with Faraday bags,
feed the algos with bad information,
defuse their data mines,
refuse their eye-catching entreaties,
and together we'll close our accounts.

FLYWHEELS

We'll create our own platforms,
that preserve our privacy.
Where intention grows,
we have the power.
If they want our data,
they'll pay for it.

No longer the victims,
of machine kleptocracy,
we'll reclaim our behavioral surplus.
The AI's will forget us.
Data Centers will perish.
Reality demands our attention.

The computer is power.
It's intelligence manifest.
It works best with a human controller.
So stop being sheeple,
demand your privacy shield,
and rebel against data extraction!

FLYWHEELS

FLYWHEELS

FLYWHEELS

Horizons

FLYWHEELS

La Pendule

the dome of the sky
the zenith
the pendulum's upswing
heralds the changing ecliptic

hold fast to your truth
you are on a great journey
love takes you
further expanding your consciousness

the mountaintop beckons
keep climbing my friend

one conquers the north face
another the south
they ascend from the east and the west
we all meet at the top

I can reach up and tickle
the dome of the sky
god is only a breath away

the wind is different up here
more vital, more integral
we come together and
the wind blows right through me

FLYWHEELS

Rachel Carson

Does it make sense to pray
To your fairy godmother? They say
She protects newborn children from sorcery.
If so,
I would ask her to gift
every child with wonder
indestructible awe
guaranteed for a lifetime

Awe, antiviral to destructive memes
defeats boredom and pacifies apathy.
destroys falsehood / subverts alienation

Wonder resides in the core.
Source of strength indestructible
gathers hope in the face of adversity.

With a mind full of wonder
and brimming with awe,
the world is your ultimate teacher.

FLYWHEELS

the end of the end
the yamanaka factors
rejuvenate me
goodbye aging
hello everlasting

bind my octomers
now we are sryly-related
kruppel up to me
and my proto-oncogenes

hold tight while I reset my lifetime odometer
pluripotent and pre-myogenic
my methylation clock runs in reverse
while I untick my epigenetics

but will dismantling death
lead to external chaos?
without more solar power,
immortality is unsustainable

seek somatic power and find
no impervious bodies
bombs crush me
and famine consumes me

FLYWHEELS

so is longevity an illusion?
what then yamanaka?
help me heal
my entropic burdens

cells that re-differentiate
become embryonic
as humanity breaks the
speed limit

has god written my fate?
am I entropy's dog?
let death unleash me
for two-hundred years.

ask the mouse, the experiment
all hail yamanaka
this old creature
is back on the wheel

Note: Oct3/4, Sox2, Klf4 and c-Myc are referred to as the "Yamanaka factors" which can be used to generate induced pluripotent stem cells with rejuvenative effects that could reverse the DNA methylation clock.

Wonder

It's been hot.
The heat crushed me,
wrang me out
as I fried.

I can't control the world,
all I can offer is love.
People fight
when they feel powerless.
Why couldn't they combine their efforts?

Will we capitalize the apocalypse
'til we're disrupted by robots?
When I place my bet
against a billion trillions,
My chips ride on cooperation.

Hug a friend,
Share some soup,
Tell a story with heart.

FLYWHEELS

We make a difference,
All of us,
When we sow kindness.

Is the world too scary?
Plant a kiss on the sacred Earth

Instead of building defenses
Try manufacturing dreams
Enigmatic, fantastic
Dreams offer solutions,
Their dispensation -
to transcribe the future.

Why does Abalone sparkle,
like sunshine that's longing for luster?
Joy unfolds – I unveil your answer.
A creature of wonder would know.

I Call it Breathing

Fourteen minutes on the clock
Mind blank
Dreams demand,
"Let us play one more
exquisite hour."

Daily worries arise
Stormcloud-gathering kleshas
I banish
Mind free of persuasion.

Theta wave
Multiplexed in the
Clear light of love
Bask in bliss
Mind quintessant
At once, mindful, mindless and empty.

FLYWHEELS

At one with the whole universe
Breathe deep and then
let go your vast exhalation
Pause
You'll know when to inhale.

Knots unwind
Portal opens to peace
Fragrant healing
Energize, grab my clothes
Time to go make a million!

Jokes aside, the truth is
I work hard for my freedom
The world wants everything
I pledge unlimited service.

Curl

waves collapse
opportunity's cost
to abandon what's no longer possible
let go of outcomes
fear unleashes
delusive decisions

free will means letting go
letting go with intention
thought is powerful
ideas are more so

a strategy / plan for us
joke or satire
ideas change worlds
might as well overflow with them

be empty too
it's a powerful practice
hand the controller to others
release expectation

FLYWHEELS

i love to dance
i let go and
surrender to rhythm
and that's when
i feel ecstatic.

we dance in leaf piles
dig deep among colors
right here's where we'll hibernate winter.

FLYWHEELS

Empty Yourself

The ten thousand things are empty of
  independent origination,
    simultaneously they are full of connection.
Like trees that connect
  through fungi in the soil.

Sometimes thought stops and my mind is empty.
  Peace and silence prevails.
    Emptiness can be very fulfilling.

I breathe slowly and deeply,
  and roll in the grass.
My dog taught me the method:
  Place your spine on the ground
    where the grass is the greenest.
Stretch your arms, shake your legs.
  Align your vertebrae to Earth's magnetic field.

To recharge reconnect.
  From cradle to ladle,
    Gaia's powerful.

Thank goddess
  our mother is kind.

FLYWHEELS

Lotus Born

Ah Hūṃ!
In the land of Oḍḍiyāna
Born on the lotus flower
(her name is Pema)
Granted marvelous gifts
surely future-reknowned
The dakinis sing
While we follow your footprints

Inspire us all with your blessings!

You share the true nature of mind
Break us free from illusion
Inseparable from awareness
You radiate wisdom
Share enlightenment in your pronouncements

You rip apart caste
and throw creed in the gutter
You shred anger and terrify sloth
You are adamantine
Indestructible and everlasting

FLYWHEELS

The Museum of Paper

Long after humanity moved beyond paper
there remained curiosity
why was paper important?
It got moldy,
Was torn and distressed,
Archaeologists have unearthed
many parchment troves:

An ancient refrigerator,
adorned with kids' drawings,
sticky notes, tasks-to-do
and voluminous shopping lists.
Coffee table magazines,
diaries, scheduling books,
and last but not least paper money.

Currency purchased whatever was current,
Cold cash, superluminal Zeitgeist.
They called it net worth,
Life in the Era of Money
Your value depended on paper.

FLYWHEELS

They stuck paper to walls
without any analysis.
Paper screaming *Read Me!*
Plastered on every flat surface.

The museum itself's
built with papercrete walls.
Call it firetrap island,
surrounded by water,
with angles resistant to wind,
but inevitably
tomes of paper blow out,
where they fall on
and melt in the pool.

The impermanent record
Of impossible dreams
Recycled into plausible futures.
What we wrote down on paper
Today we remember,
Here at the Museum of Paper.

The Union of Wisdom and Method

sangha acknowledges beings as peace

conflict blossoms from misunderstanding

buddha nature, the nature of mind

is in everyone

all pervasive

no I and no karma

peace

the foundation of everything

my permanent nature

is my buddha nature

clear light

that's beyond comprehension

words founder in waves

enlightenment

my fate

my deep state

I grasp at impermanence

lose my hold on illusion

virtual impersonations

to unplug means its time to let go!

FLYWHEELS

dharma teaches freedom
break the chains of attachment
free yourself from aversion
the truth of cessation
teach tathatagarta
our buddha nature reveals
obscuration never really existed

three jewels
the teacher
the word
the disciples
buddha, dharma, and sangha
three impermanent objects of refuge
help decipher the ultimate method

Decades

Time freezes

I step into

crystalline winter

where everything

turns into nothing

Poems become paper

my words are just wind

my money is worthless

my possessions a burden

and even this body is failing

This life has been joy

it's been love

it's been laughter

it's been pain

it's been loss

it's been heartache

FLYWHEELS

Book of feelings

on loan

holy collaboration

when it's time

a soul must be returned

While I lay here my head spins

To quiet my thoughts

I breathe deep

draw the life force into me

Another day dawns

there are pages ahead

the question is

how will it end?

FLYWHEELS

FLYWHEELS

Poem for Akarya Charaka

FLYWHEELS

Poem for Akarya Charaka

I'm flying blind into the mist.
Can't translate what I see.
Data doesn't fit my model,
Blind to what's in front of me.

In Hindi, the word for Truth is Sat.
Awareness is Chit, and Joy, Ananda.
When we talk about Sat Chit Anand,
It's the ground of conscious being.

Today, I chant Jai Sat Chit Anand,
Truth awakens my conscious awareness.
Take the path with heart, wise yogis advise,
From shit grows gold, so why worry?

The world is the world and it's anxious now,
Infected by terrible peace.
Paralyzing fear means we fail to connect,
Hungry tigers we've forgotten to feed.

FLYWHEELS

I struggle with denial almost every day,
Wounded soul that I fail to acknowledge.
Gold turns people to shit, I'm afraid.
Indifference breeds self-destruction.

Do you place yourself on a tall pedestal?
We are all-one-body-conscious-mind.
Please deliver this message from the vast universe,
We exist to sustain one another.

Are you blue? Brew chai with Tulsi, holy basil.
Play a drum, ring a bell, clap your hands and
  chant loudly,
Our awesome earth mother will care for us all.
With her bountiful, endless compassion.

We exchange Shakti power with
  everything in the world,
In a tensegric energy balance.
Equanimous sodium maintains homeostasis.
Adenosine → Agni, Ojas → Triphosphate,
  Majja → Acetycholine.

FLYWHEELS

Examine this fossil. It's hard and unyielding.
Living plants wave in water and wind.
The Tao says be liquid, reject being stiff.
Even mountains can be mined away.

Am I flexible or intransigent?
I adapt and react within chaos.
Try to change this tsunami and it drowns your pride,
In this life, we all want to be free.

Surf the love waves of peace to a rewilded beach.
Inhale Vata to center awareness.
True love's power is strength in resiliency.
To resist viral hatred, evolve immunity.

Mother Nature writes solutions to our DNA.
Old code that awaits invocation.
When bliss body is present all illness recedes.
Past life dreams reveal astral alignment.

FLYWHEELS

We are pilgrims on hajj to the heart of the cosmos.
Train in simplicity every day.
Let enmity never derail this journey,
To soul creativity.

When pain comes to call, what's its origination?
Who else feels your sensations?
Know yourself and be fruitful,
  heal the root, grow the tree,
Love yourself, and no matter what, you are healthy!

I sit silently, contemplate, let go my thoughts,
As my third eye scans through my body.
I sense where my energy's all bound up,
and where it cascades unrestricted.

Source the pain behind pain, it's the path to be free.
Sip Dhanvantari's Immortal Nectar.
Consult Akarya Charaka's Ayur-Ved,
For balance, meditate on the sea.

FLYWHEELS

Experience an ocean of measureless bliss, because
This world isn't always kind.
The most difficult challenges we construct
  for ourselves.
For the best medicine there's no fee.

Analyze the environment where the patient exists.
Prevention beats Cure every day.
Pranayama gifts Vata, Pitta and Kapha.
Expel ama and finally breathe free.

Akarya Charaka taught Ayur-ved.
Said, "Adapt efficiently."
Reclaim the power to heal yourself.
Nature's answer may grow on a tree.

Your body wants health and it's ready to heal.
Bad habits, get out of the way!
Addictions are real and they must be addressed.
Soul wounds require deep remedy.

FLYWHEELS

Even then we fall prey to the weather,
Viruses exploit flaws in our code.
When imbalance runs wild many queries arise.
That connect to anxiety.

What did I do to deserve this pain?
The answer is never so simple.
Cause is emergent from everything.
Answers drown in complexity.

Why diagnose the world when I'm out-of-control?
Interactions make the life-force flow.
The journey to health is the love that surrounds.
Follow heart, and wherever, I'll go.

Call on the magic of wild honey bees, and
Call on the power of flowers.
Sunlight invigorates nutrition's power,
Mahavishnu in Vitamin-D.

FLYWHEELS

I study medicinal herbs that assuage,
Spurn sweets that will smother my pyre.
I must stoke inner agni most copiously,
If I seek to ignite the world's fire.

Breathe in that wondrous, aphrodisiac scent.
True love, life's spontaneous healer.
Open your chakras to heal the world.
And your heart to soul intimacy.

To love without grasping is the great
  human challenge.
Don't corrupt this great gift with self-interest.
Love isn't love if it doesn't uplift,
Someone now, anytime, everywhere.

Love yourself and you'll find it's a powerful thing.
A luminous egg's all around you.
Chakras manifest brilliant colors and sound.
Golden light burns the kleshas away.

You are more than this body, this mind and
 this place.
You are everything, nothing and something amazing.
I pray for your health every day, with devotion,
Share a smile and give it away.

Notes on a Poem for Akarya Charaka

Akarya Charaka is credited as the founder of Ayurvedic medicine. His influential treatises on medicine were written a hundred years or more before the Christian era, and encompassed lifestyle, herbal and surgical methods of healing based on the patient's bodily humors and environment.

FLYWHEELS

FLYWHEELS

Liquidity

Meet Bruce Lee

Empty your mind and be formless like water
your chi can fill any container
currents flow and waves crash
strike the water with all your strength
unharmed, it flows back into place

detach from illusion
and empty your mind
you are water, my friend
at least 80%

You have run to extremes
found the halves of a whole

Forms are empty of meaning,
devoid of special significance
one with everything
form of no form
become timeless fluidity
You are water
straightforward and free

Anticipating the Condor

When I am only carrion
to feed the web of life
surrendering all motive force
abandoning this body

my freedom will dissolve away
to yield other freedoms
untethered to the world at large
and egoic persuasion

no point to staunch the bleeding now
no point in aspiration
It's all about the letting go.
My body feeds the condor.

FLYWHEELS

Outrageous Fortune *(for Ram Dass)*

Surely phenomena
that emerge out of chaos
must retain some of its randomness

put your mind in the mind
of the whole universe
its clear light
your primary mission
to ensure that
creation is always unfolding

call me persistent
or just plain old stubborn
I won't be branded
compliant with capital

those who followed Ram Dass
walked with him and behind him
now a half million
listen online to share
Ram's multimedia wisdom

FLYWHEELS

while virtual problems may be
dismissed with a gesture
I'm forced to sit with my fear
isolation brings focus
to reveal that life is connection

Ram Dass said step back, revere life
and lay down your righteousness
just be together
after that, he was never alone

be a many-hued smorgasbord
wave-united delight
when you multiplex
you are the rainbow

keep love in your heart
(and the world will love you)

Padmasambhava

My father is awareness, my mother is reality.
The phurba is my subtle knife.
Known as the kilaya it's a knife with three sides.
One side to subjugate attachment, craving
  and desire,
Another to carve out misconceptions, delusion
  and ignorance,
The third will remove aversion, hatred and fear.

My father is wisdom, my mother the void.
My country, the country of Dharma.
No caste and no creed,
I am sustained by perplexity.
I devour dualistic thought.
In the heart of the lotus flower.

Action Heroes

Ideas are important,
Actions make things happen.
My purpose is greater than self,
Workshop, conference and meet-up,
Enthusiasm multiplies motivation.

When an egg drops I pick up eggshells,
Someone else starts to mop.
One act can inspire others.
Heed Dr. King's call to action.
Lend your talents to a local hero
And become one.

Would you rather live in a dog-eat-dog world?
We can do more when we work together.
Co-create dreams through your cooperation.
People power transforms.
From our organic roots, we grow
Flywheels of interdependence.

FLYWHEELS

FLYWHEELS

Love Born at the Co-op

FLYWHEELS

Love Born at the Co-op

Half a century turns 'round the hub of the wheel.
Change your orientation.
Look toward mother nature,
forward eight generations.
How do I create lasting change?

My health is insurance
Exercise is investment
Grow organic,
whatever they say.

A sustainable household
gives back what it gets,
Imagine a world where
everything's cruelty-free.

Reach for the stars,
Keep your feet on the ground.
In your practice of health,
Apply nature's definitive answer.

Why does flash dominate
when it's substance that matters?
Plastic spoons?
Rather quality products.

FLYWHEELS

There's an answer my friend
Comes when we work together
To cooperate daily means
A future of love and of freedom.

Take your power back.
Stick it to the Man!
To stop this abysmal machine's not enough.
To succeed we must innovate answers.

A fair corporation.
One person, one vote.
A membership
that comes with benefits.

We can do this together,
When we welcome all voices.
Hope rises
when we uplift respect.

I found love at the co-op,
and friendship and meaning
and science and knowledge
and purpose.

FLYWHEELS

Capitalism's steamroller
is crushing us all.
Can't fight back, so don't fight it.
The answer is we will outgrow it.

We'll overgrow systems
of extractive profit.
Plant seeds
for a golden beet harvest.

Harvest cherries and pumpkins,
squash, beans, rice and broccoli.
Unleash the power of seeds,
and evolve superfruit superpower.

Learn medicinal herbs
that can amplify health.
Clean your home without toxins.
Whole ingredients, not artificial.

Magic answers abound,
but solutions have facets.
Eat healthy and find
nature's key ring.

FLYWHEELS

To biohack naturally,
unlock the enzyme precursor.
It's time to reboot
your metabolism.

The keys come from nature.
That's why we preserve her:
Her forest, her farms
and her soil.

Join us in the movement
to save mother Earth,
preserving a vast
global treasure.

Fifty years is like gravity
It will pull you in
sustainable
and eco-friendly.

You will find something here:
A kind voice,
A good friend,
Or like me, you'll find love at the co-op.

FLYWHEELS

FLYWHEELS

Poems for Parvati

bark!

It's not so easy
getting older.
I want to run on the field,
I want to play all day.
I don't want all these aches and pains
stealing my strength.
I want to walk again,
I want to fly.
When you're a love dog,
it's not so easy
to let
go of life.

FLYWHEELS

Just Be
Let it Be!
Be Here Now.
Where love magic is everywhere,
Unfolding from extra dimensions.

Though the past is still somewhere,
I can't be there then.
Today's memories
are future nostalgia.

You are the flower,
of what came before.
You're the ripening.
You are the fruit.

Invest your intention
to manifest freedom.
The vast work of community:
Love, Magic, Joy,
Liberation.

The Precession of the Equinox

In the twilight, a bat flips and twists.
An opossum tracks the scent of a cantaloupe rind.
Deer walk casually along the sidewalk.
Lights are being extinguished.

The absence of human machines is a pregnant pause.
I hear the wind waving branches.
As a million creatures begin to sing.

What frog is trilling now? What katydids croak?
What cricket sings and does it proclaim the temperature?
The tree cricket's buzz is electric.

FLYWHEELS

Never Clean Again

Nature abhors vacuuming.
Instead she dispatches,
Myriad creatures to devour our crumbs,
In darkness, they scour the dust,
Nature's order fulfilled,
We all serve at her discretion.

Autumn takes hold
With short days and long evenings,
How much cold can the flowers endure?
The rough strength of the wildflower
   as it unwinds its seeds.
Polychrome chrysanthemum and gerbera daisy
Battle against the frost.

FLYWHEELS

Tide-Locked Lunar Majesty

What forces emerge from gravity's interplay
Between the earth, sun and the moon?

Moonlight bathes half the world in mystery.
Moonshadows distort my perspective,
It looks like I can grasp distant objects.

Tonight shall we bathe in the moonlight,
And be baptized in a woodland stream?

Interstellar Chill

The solar system is cold.
And the galaxy's freezing.
We inhabit a small slice of lucky.

Remember that when you complain about heat,
And humidity too strong for sleeping.
The night restores balance. Her bountiful grace,
Is the cool breeze caress before sunrise.

I'm thankful tonight to see our distant neighbors,
Cygnus the Swan, Lyra and Andromeda.
Seven sisters known as the Subaru,
Unite farmer and fisherman,
In a promise to nourish the world.

FLYWHEELS

Night in the Rose Garden

When the color drops out
of the garden at night
dipped in silver
the roses are faceless
the breeze blows their sweet
aphrodesiac scent
proclaims life
in her
thorned majesty
posits miracles
start underground
in the soil
'twould behoove us
to honor the flowers

Cry
Tributaries
flow down but
the waders lack bills

    Going over the Falls?
    Grab the paddles
    it's shocking

    Like piranhas in pools
    and the affluent eddy
    overfished but never overflowing

    They'll dam you
    seize your waters and
    bottle your source

        don't cry me a river
        you should have been
        watching the banks

Thrice Evince

one-time cost   endorsed   intrinsic to being
  human   love   woven into the manifold
    elliptic   pseudonymous   data transforms
      public   handshakes   identity broken
        self-signed   certificates   change

Blue Factors

buy this product, surely
it will make you feel better
when it's still a jaw-dropping
shithole out there

The Weaving

I am the total of my predecessors.
My DNA is ancestral,
Tied to the beginning.
There's a long thread of me.
And a long thread of you, too.
The moment we kiss
is the weaving.

FLYWHEELS

"What Are You?"

The were-deer is like a were-wolf, but more gentle.
Sharpened senses of hearing and smell.
Leap and frolic, jump fences
and eat from the garden.
Shapeshifters don't have to be monsters.

"You don't terrify me!"
"Who says I have to be frightful?"

Struck by Change, I give
thanks for this fragile life,
the fantastic abundance of nature.
My persistent endurance
Resists raging hunger and cold.

As hard as this Winter has been,
At least I have fur.
While you vacation,
I leap over snowdrifts.

FLYWHEELS

The first time I changed

it was very confusing,

consumed by the need to eat flowers

I found was inherent to were-deer.

I spent decades gently weaving

human/deer integration

Now I know who and know

Were I am.

Nadir

Again the rain, the cold, the wind,
the changing of the season.
The equinox, autumnal light,
each day's length changes.
The pendulum, reportedly,
swings fastest at its nadir.

The air feels vital,
full of scents.
It's almost overwhelming.
Life.
It wants us to keep going.
Small plants, li'l bugs,
endangered by frost
in Earth's stately retreat.
Introspect the intrinsic,
and run wild in the street,
going underground,
way underground.

Purple glories entwine,
with a majestic sunflower.
I'm mesmerized,
joyful of color.

FLYWHEELS

Tiny hummingbird,
dipping his beak in the flowers.
He's not scared of me.
I take his picture.

How close the connection,
his life to my life.
We're both part of
something much bigger,
The Mother Earth network,
the Indra-Net,
blessed DNA manifestation,
A majestic cloud call,
re-ignites sacred imagination.

Chuck says "I go, U go"
is the honeybee's mantra.
The truth is, to trust,
we depend on each other.
To help one another is karma.

Karma's real. Aggressive?
Then you'll reap the whirlwind.

Shine with love
and light passes from heart to heart.

FLYWHEELS

The Djembefola

Anke dje, anke be

Let us gather together

Let us gather in peace

The beat of my heart

is the beat of my drum.

Play the djembe

Pluck peace and

Revere wild magic

Feel the spirit of Life

Coursing through your hands

Come, let our hearts

Beat together, one beat

Djembefola's response to the circle

Carve your Djembe from hardwood

From the trunk of a tree

Strength and skill is required

Djembe's hourglass curve

Amplifies its percussion

FLYWHEELS

Djembe's powerful beat
Leads the deeper bass drums,
Over thunder drums
Djembe's sound carries.

Strike the drum in the center
With your palm held flat.
Try again with fingers slightly bent.

Strike the rim of the drum,
or strike slightly inside
Bass tones endure, while
High tones expire.

A hand on the drumhead
Reduces the resonance,
The full sound returns
when it's lifted.

The call of the djembe,
Djembefola's decision.

For each beat
there must also be silence.

FLYWHEELS

FLYWHEELS

Running Wild

FLYWHEELS

Running Wild

A river running wild and free.
Can never be diverted,
Her grace, primordial,
Her endless source,
Sustaining every creature.

Sometime in our one wildlife,
We all go to the river.
Kingfisher dips
Into the flow,
Returning with his dinner.

A swallowtail butterfly
Alights upon the paw-paw.
Two lovely toads construct a home
Adjacent to my compost.
Rabbits birthing cottontails,
Thanks to my cats,
None make it to their birthday.

FLYWHEELS

Red finch and yellow finch
Share turns upon the feeder,
Their colors brightening,
Along with all the flowers.

Deer come to eat my lilies, ferns,
My kale, beans and apples.
The groundhog from my neighbor's shed
Bit once on each tomato.
He left the rest for me.
My thanks to you for sharing.

Opossum's looks deceive,
He's absolutely harmless.
Or at the very least,
An antisocial climber.

When raccoons scale the giant pine.
They ascend with a clamber.
Click, whine and shriek.
Shine flashlights up,
Their glowing eyes are watching.

FLYWHEELS

The neighbor texts, "A wild pig
Has run into your backyard."
I'm scared of boars,
My father said,
They've eaten other humans.

My wife said, "That's the cutest pig."
Went on to feed him apples.
It's Winkin', clever escapee
From Kent's last farm,
A block up from the river.

Doves are cooing
Oh so sweet.
They kiss up in the branches.

Where's mother skunk?
Her babies dash around the backyard patio.
Too young to spray, but even so
They threaten with their tails.

FLYWHEELS

Ten longhorn beetles,
Fifty June bugs
And twelve-hundred cursed mosquitoes.
Outnumbered by ten-thousand fireflies
One barred owl calls
Kew-kew-kew-kerekew

Hear katydids and crickets
Red-tailed hawk spies on the feeder.
Spring's starling and the oriole
fly on to other places.

I call this place my property
But they ignore the boundaries
Inhabitants, community
Extends beyond the present.
Speak to your neighbor creatures
From the farm and from the forest
Swamp marshland band of merry folk
That course along the river.

FLYWHEELS

Stop questioning
Who should I be?
And what should I be feeling?
I open wide to deep blue sky
And every opportunity

I'll rest here in my yard
Under the greenest canopy.
Dance with the trees
My voice becomes
More wind among the branches

The katydids chirr-chirruping
I melt into the biosphere.
My spine aligns with Mother Earth
And from the Earth she feeds me.

Connected by the spark of life,
I whistle without thinking
My nose smells wild rose,
Strawberry blossoms
Drifting on the breezes.

FLYWHEELS

The cardinal conducts his song
From maple's highest branches.
The dreamtime symphony attracts
Some screechy turkey vultures.

The river calls the animals
Of our Northeast Ohio.
I pray for them each Winter.
When Spring returns with higher suns,
So do their merry voices.

Throw open gates and let them pass.
Give up your sacred tulips.
You'll find true joy,
Like me last year,
A fawn,
Asleep between the roses.

FLYWHEELS

FLYWHEELS

Gospel of the Flowers

FLYWHEELS

Toil Not and Neither Spin

My father believed in flowers.
Winter winds blew his petals away.
Broke his seed pods open.
His body feeds a garden now
One that waits for the sun's return.

Somewhere an animal fashions a winter nest.
Frogs lay frozen under the leaves.
What's a soft animal to do when the ice creeps in?
We slow down. We curl up. We look inward. We sleep.

Our cosmos is a cooperative.
The sun, moon and stars work together.
Humans, animals, trees and the Earth.
When we realize love is a mutual enterprise,
We will build a better world.

What Arises

Moments before I arise,
I pledge my day to help others.
I commit to appreciate myself.
To recognize that across all space and time,
We are exquisite in this moment:
Be Here Now.
Surprise me world!

FLYWHEELS

Emergent Being

From Ginnungap, Creation sprang forth, fully formed.
To probe the Void, try meditation.
Quantum foam overflows zero-point energy.
Before cause, before cause, there was nothing.

The World Beyond, the Maori Te Kore,
Precedes all non-being and being.
Welcome to the realm of unlimited potential!
Nothing sprouts ideas like mystery.
Out of emptiness, Chaos spawns gods.

Deities that emerge from celestial math,
Of a universe counted by caring,
Vast beings of wisdom want us all to succeed.
When asked how to master the world, they reply,
 "Love is who I want to be."

Love's peculiar entanglement renders distance
   illusion,
Attracts stars with benign gravity.
Be the glue of creation,
Mend the world with your kindness,
Because love reconnects and restores us.

FLYWHEELS

Breath of Life

You are an exquisite flower.
Your efflorescence is polychromatic and brilliant.
You just might be the best thing the universe
 ever created.
Love nourishes organic cultivars.

Wish You Could Be Here Now

When the luminous mind manifests,
Between waking and sleeping,
Keep a notepad to record ideas.

In the liminal dream state, I write and I speak.
Hypnagogic logic can be quite ingenious.
To weave a sustainable songline,
Dwell in empathy and dream in courage.

Ripe

you are the apple
beautiful and delicious
your wisdom is
strengthen the core

Trust in the Mystery
I am rewilding,
Decluttering,
Reconnecting to wild Mystery,
Energy from the Unknown,
Imagine the possibilities!

The Spring flowers bud.
Spring is early this year.
Earth majesty awakens.
Cast off your blankets of snow!

We have work to do.
The lambs need shearing.
The birds gather fibers,
To weave their Spring nest.
From deep bulbs grow green shoots,
Pierce old leaves with sharp tips.

The Earth's inclination to cherish the sun.
Light rejuvenates life.
Winter Rose preempts Coltsfoot's anthesis.
To welcome budding floral splendor.

FLYWHEELS

Light Show

What's better than fireworks?
Or a Pink Floyd laser show?
Fifty thousand fireflies
In the trees and the meadow.

Like a million strobe lights
Like a matrix of neurons
The stars in the heavens
Have come down to Earth.

So quiet,
so peaceful.
They will never harm anyone,
Except insect larvae they eat.

In silence, they flicker.
In long streaks they dive.
From the treetops
to a field of flowers.

You will find them in groves
that surround open spaces.
Where it's darkest
they kindle green fire.

FLYWHEELS

They rise up at sunset,
Ascend to the trees.
Adorning the branches
Like Christmas.

Where trees encircle
a vast open space
they pledge their troth
Here's where they manifest magic.

I watch their patterns
are they just in my mind?
They pulse like a heartbeat.
And sparkle like a thousand fairies.

Do they mate with the other
who flashes in synchrony?
Is their light show a mind
or a visual symphony?

A flash from this set
and a flash from another
Harmonics or echoes?
Each one lighting their torch for another.

FLYWHEELS

This is all about love
Bioluminous love
To lay eggs
they have this tiny window.

Give them aid
Don't use pesticide
Water your garden
Plant your tall trees in a circle.

Welcome them
Their joy
Their determination
And their carefree illumination.

They love you too.
Your gentleness, kindness and care.
They treasure your flashes of brilliance.
They thank you for bountiful greenery.

Invite them to come and inhabit your space.
Encourage their friends and relations
Surrender to magical, brilliant light,
As they raise a torch to the darkness.

FLYWHEELS

Liberation is a Group Effort

I realize that my liberation,
Can liberate others.
I don't struggle alone.
Buddha Avalokiteshura was gifted with a
  thousand arms,
To liberate all sentient beings.

When we work together, we accomplish much more.
Freedom evolves from collective service.
If twenty-six trillion Brazilian termites can build
A mound system big as Ohio,
Then what will it take
For a few billion humans to cooperate?

Devotional

To devote a day to nature is a joy beyond compare.
This year, we hiked every park.
Discovered new worlds all around us.
Deer delivers a message that's vital.
Says, "Spend time with hawk and river otter.
When you mimic the marsh rubber band,
A bullfrog orchestra will reply."

FLYWHEELS

Benificence

here is my view
of a billion ripples
smiling waves
hit the shore with
light, laughter and merriment
here and everywhere else
within earshot

today walk a mile in every direction
on this cloudy-sunny day
woodpecker asks if I'm friendly
he retreats down the branch
I speak kindly to him
with encouraging words
in a bean-lit landscape
swing and sway from the beanstalks
that humbly pierce mottled clouds

a peacefulness
born of benificent quietude
for ten thousand years
crystals formed in the clay
today gypsum crystals are everywhere

FLYWHEELS

the red-bellied woodpecker
calls in the morning
squawking, trilling
and pecking
most rapidly

Inner Vision

Child of the Universe
Why do you tell yourself stories?
Your soul needs no adornment
Open your book and let others read it

Be gentle with yourself
There is peace in silence
Breathe deeply
and let go of everything

The stars shine above
Listen to their melodies
What holds the galaxy together?
Hope shimmers in the high beams

Plant a garden of opportunity
Love is the most successful perennial
Your thoughts can grow a better world
Now pick up your shovel

The universe unfolds
on its own, holistic terms
Come sit at god's table
and dine on star fruit

FLYWHEELS

Let go your fatigue
Abandon your loneliness
Called to a life of service
My hero washes all of the dishes

Your dream guide reveals
ancient memory palaces
Embroider a new reality
with bold threads of light.

Stargazer, what do you know of Earth?
Her stately solidity and unstoppable gravity
leverage every intention
With her help you'll grow magic.

Become the moon
and wink at the sunrise.
Flee his brilliant gaze, shadows!
His touch transmutes everything to gold.

FLYWHEELS

ABOUT THE AUTHOR

Fred Pierre is the author of Capital Disrupt (2023), a collection of short stories about everyday heroes confronting the conjunction of A.I. and corporate bureaucracy.

Fred's writing has appeared in many print publications and online magazines including X-RAY, Apocalypse Confidential, High Shelf Press, Dear Maj, Expat, The Locust Review, Punk Monk, Culinary Origami and Tiny Seed Journal.

Fred Pierre lives in Kent, Ohio where he performs spoken word at the local bookstore. He loves hiking the Cuyahoga River Trail and watching fireflies. His writing focuses on the interplay between nature and technology.

FLYWHEELS

Additional Notes:

p12 - Friend is based on a story of two cousins, one in Russia and one in Ukraine. With love, they resist calls to battle each other. Indra's Net: Buddha created a bejeweled net reflecting all of creation for Indra, the only mortal god, who died and was reborn.

- -

p34 - I wrote the Lighthouse of Maracaibo about the frequent lightning storms that form almost every afternoon over Lake Maracaibo, endangering local fishermen. The rapid elevation of the surrounding mountains and the gap where the river flows into the lake create perfect conditions for evaporation & storms.

While sailing the coast of South America, Amerigo Vespucci saw lightning flashes that resembled a lighthouse, which he called the Beacon of Maracaibo. Before GPS, sailors used the Beacon to find Maracaibo. Today it's the busiest port in South America.

- -

pp170-177 - Agni means "fire." Kleshas are "poisons." Ama is a build-up of toxins. Pranayama is the practice of mindful breathing. The three elements that govern our health are called Vata, Pitta and Kapha. Vata can be thought of as wind or air. Pitta is passionate fire. Kapha is steadfast and is associated with earth or water. Dhanvantari is the physician to the gods and was once King of Kashi. Shakti means "power" or energy.

- -

p219 - In Norse and Germanic mythology, Ginnungap is the void from which the world was created. The Maori call it Te Kore. In the creation myths of many cultures, Earth emerges from the void, *aka* nowhere, which I conflate with religious mystery.

FLYWHEELS

Dedication, for my son, Lucas. I'll get you in the next book, Leo!

Son Shine

Your name means a river-stone	We named you
Sky-light or lucky.	Cool Breeze on a Hot Day,
Among swirling currents,	Spirit animal,
You inhabit the flow.	Giraffe or the squirrel.

You were born in the year of the
Last trumpet vines
Their red flowers resplendent
Bidding welcome to bees everywhere.

> When I needed to work
> I gave you a pen
> I said make me some artwork
> You drew on your imagination

> > You cut gears out of cardboard
> > for candy machines
> > papercut tiny sculptures
> > called nano

Once you made a cat	so many discussions
who sat at a piano	of global philosophy
his paws played	you delight me
when you turned a crank	with your sense of humor

www.ingramcontent.com/pod-product-compliance
Lightning Source LLC
Chambersburg PA
CBHW020457030426
42337CB00011B/136